AUG 2 2 2007

THE EMERGENCE OF SOCIAL COGNITION IN THREE YOUNG CHIMPANZEES

Michael Tomasello
Malinda Carpenter

WITH COMMENTARY BY
R. Peter Hobson

Willis F. Overton
Series Editor

MONOGRAPHS OF THE SOCIETY FOR RESEARCH IN CHILD DEVELOPMENT

Serial No. 279, Vol. 70, No. 1, 2005

RETA E. KING LIBRARY
CHADRON STATE COLLEGE
CHADRON, NE 69337

Blackwell Publishing

Boston, Massachusetts   Oxford, United Kingdom

156
T591e

EDITOR
WILLIS F. OVERTON
Temple University

EDITORIAL ASSISTANT
MARGARET BERRY
Temple University

CONSULTING EDITORS FOR THE MONOGRAPHS (2005)

William Arsenio
Wesleyan University

Rebecca Bigler
University of Texas-Austin

Peg Burchinal
University of North Carolina, Chapel Hill

Susan Campbell
University of Pittsburgh

Stephanie Carlson
University of Washington

W. Andrew Collins
University of Minnesota

Kenneth Dodge
Duke University

William Dukowski
Corcordia University

Nancy Eisenberg
Arizona State University

Nancy Galambos
University of Alberta

Shaun Gallagher
University of Central Florida

Susan Gelman
University of Michigan

Elizabeth Gershoff
Columbia University

Thomas Gould
Temple University

Joan Grusec
University of Toronto

Steven Guberman
University of Colorado

Jeffrey J. Haugaard
Cornell University

R. Peter Hobson
Tavistock Clinic
Development psychopathology Research Unit
London, England

Tim Ingold
University of Aberdeen, United Kingdom

Andrew Karpinski
Temple University

Robert Larzeler
University of Nebraska

Campbell Leaper
University of California, Santa Cruz

Suniya Luthar
Columbia University

Peter Marshall
Temple University

Constance Milbrath
University of California, San Francisco

Lou Moses
University of Oregon

Ulrich Mueller
University of Victoria
Victoria, Canada

Larry Nucci
University of Illinois at Chicago

Sue Parker
Sonoma University

Gregory S. Petit
Auburn University

Paul Quinn
University of Delaware

Karen Saywitz
Harbor UCLA Medical School

Bryan Sokol
Simon Fraser University

Elizabeth Vandewater
University of Texas, Austin

David Wolfe
Center for Addiction & Mental Health
London, Ontario, CA

Hongling Xie
Temple University

THE EMERGENCE OF SOCIAL COGNITION IN THREE YOUNG CHIMPANZEES

CONTENTS

COMMENTARY

ABSTRACT

We report a series of 10 studies on the social-cognitive abilities of three young chimpanzees. The studies were all ones previously conducted with human infants. The chimpanzees were 1–5 years of age, had been raised mostly by humans, and were tested mostly directly by a familiar human experimenter.

First, in a longitudinal investigation with repeated measurements from a social-cognitive test battery, the three young chimpanzees were similar in many ways to human infants; the major difference was a total lack of attempts to share attention with others either in joint attentional interactions or through declarative gestures. Second, in imitation-based tests of the understanding of intentional action, the chimpanzees, like human infants, showed an understanding of failed attempts and accidents; but they did not pay attention to the behavioral style of the actor or the actor's reasons for choosing a particular behavioral means. Third, in tests of their understanding of visual perception, the chimpanzees followed the gaze direction of a human to an out-of-sight location behind a barrier and gestured more to a human who could see them than to one who could not; but they showed no understanding that perceivers can focus their attention on one thing, or one aspect of a thing, within their perceptual fields for a reason. Finally, in tests of joint intentions and joint attention, the chimpanzees showed no ability to either reverse roles with a partner in a collaborative interaction or to set up a joint attentional framework for understanding the communicative intentions behind a pointing gesture.

Taken together, these findings support the idea that the early ontogeny of human social cognition comprises two distinct trajectories, each with its own evolutionary history: one for understanding the basics of goal-directed action and perception, common to all apes, and another for sharing psychological states with others in collaborative acts involving joint intentions and attention, unique to the human species.

I. INTRODUCTION

In 1976, Nicolas Humphrey looked at his laboratory monkeys and all of the clever things they were doing in experiments and asked, in effect, why are they so smart? Navigating and foraging in the physical world is not so much more complex for primates than for other mammals, and yet they seem so much brighter. Humphrey (1976) observed that in their daily lives the most complex things primates do involve navigating not their physical worlds but their social worlds, as they compete with and try to outwit other individuals who are at the same time competing with and trying to outwit them. This "social function of intellect" hypothesis has generated much research in the last three decades demonstrating that, indeed, a major reason for primates' relatively large brains and sophisticated cognitive skills is the complex social worlds in which they operate (e.g., Byrne & Whiten, 1988; de Waal, 1982; Tomasello & Call, 1997).

The human primate seems to have gone even further in this direction. Perhaps more than any other species, human beings live complex social lives in which they must navigate through the goals, intentions, perceptions, thoughts, beliefs, desires, and opinions of their fellow human beings. And in some accounts, the complex social-cognitive skills required for this social navigation are also responsible for the unique social organization of human beings, most often called "culture" (Tomasello, Kruger, & Ratner, 1993). Human cultural organization is responsible for creating over historical time the complex material and symbolic artifacts (including language) that amplify so dramatically individual human-cognitive skills, and that structure so thoroughly the cognitive ontogeny of developing human children (Vygotsky, 1978).

The social-cognitive skills that underlie human culture emerge in two major steps in human ontogeny. Best known is the transformation that occurs in children's social reasoning at around 4 years of age. It is at this age that children are able to deal for the first time with beliefs as major determinants of human action. Thus, it is only at 4 years of age that children are able to predict that someone who desires a toy and believes that it is in

1

the cupboard will search in the cupboard, even though the toy is really under the sofa (Wimmer & Perner, 1983). Children of this age thus operate with something resembling an adult belief–desire psychology in which people intentionally pursue their goals based not on reality, but on their beliefs about reality (Perner, 1991; Wellman, 1990). This understanding enables school-aged children to have at least some comprehension of the most complex human cultural creations such as money, marriage, and government, which exist because and only because of the collective practices and beliefs of some group of people.

Less well-known and researched is the first major ontogenetic step in human social cognition at around 1 year of age when infants begin to perceive the actions and perceptions of other persons in intentional terms in the first place. It is at this tender age that infants for the first time begin to see what others are doing not just as bodily motions but as goal-directed actions and perceptions. Daddy is not just moving his arms in certain ways but he is trying to open the drawer. Mommy is not just turning her head in a direction but she is attending to some particular aspect of her perceptual field relevant to her current goals. Understanding others in this way, as intentional agents, is the foundation for all other forms of social understanding in the sense that we actually define what a person is doing by the goals she is trying to achieve (Tomasello, 1995).

As infants begin understanding others in this way they begin doing all kinds of things that are unique to the species, involving many different kinds of cultural, collaborative, and symbolic activities. Tomasello (1999) therefore proposed that 1-year-olds' perception–goal psychology (understanding others as attentional and intentional agents like the self) was both a necessary and sufficient social-cognitive foundation for children's initial entry into culture. Recently, however, research has emerged suggesting that our nearest primate relatives, the great apes, may possess more social-cognitive skills than previously believed, including especially the understanding of others' goals and perceptions (Tomasello, Call, & Hare, 2003). But because apes' ability to create and participate in cultural conventions and institutions is clearly not human-like, there must be some additional factor in human cognition. Based on a review of the existing empirical data, Tomasello, Carpenter, Call, Behne, and Moll (in press) hypothesized that this additional factor is what philosophers of action call shared intentionality. Shared intentionality, sometimes called "we" intentionality, refers to collaborative interactions in which participants have a shared goal (shared commitment) and coordinated action roles for pursuing that shared goal (Gilbert, 1989; Tuomela, 1995; Searle, 1995; Bratman, 1992). The proposal is thus that what makes human social/cultural cognition unique is not how individuals understand the actions of others per se, but rather how they then engage with others in various forms of shared intentionality involving joint action, joint attention, and symbolic communication (Tomasello & Rakoczy, 2003). Engaging in acts of shared intentionality requires both a special motivation to share psychological states with others and some form of dialogic cognitive representation for doing so.

Tomasello et al. (in press) thus hypothesized that the ontogeny of human social cognition was a product of the interaction of two developmental trajectories, each representing an evolutionary adaptation from some different point in time. The first trajectory is a general primate (or perhaps great ape) line of development for understanding intentional action and perception, which evolved in the context of primates' crucially important competitive interactions with one another over food, mates, and other resources (Machiavellian intelligence; Byrne & Whiten, 1988). The second trajectory is a uniquely human line of development for sharing psychological states with others in acts of shared intentionality. When and how this evolved is not known, but one hypothesis is that it emerged in the last 150,000 years as a result of selection pressures favoring the new forms of cultural organization and symbolic communication characteristic of modern humans. The interaction of these two lines of development creates uniquely human forms of social cognition, which in turn make possible uniquely human forms of cultural cognition, learning, and creation.

One way to test this hypothesis—or at least some aspects of it—would be to look more closely at the ontogeny of social cognition in our nearest primate relatives. In this *Monograph*, therefore, we explore the early social cognition of one of our two closest primate relatives, the chimpanzee. We do this through a series of studies with three young chimpanzees who were raised with much interaction with humans and their artifacts. The studies were mostly designed after ones previously conducted with human infants at around 1 year of age, and so they focus on the degree to which, and the ways in which, these chimpanzees might share the perception–goal psychology and the forms of shared intentionality that first emerge in humans at this age. We thus look at the ability of these young chimpanzees (a) to understand and reproduce the intentional actions of others, (b) to understand the perceptions and attention of others, and (c) to share intentions and attention with others in various joint attentional, collaborative, and communicative interactions. Our goal is to sketch a kind of primate (or great ape) baseline from which human social cognition differentiated itself at some point in the 5–6 million years during which humans have been on their own evolutionary trajectory.

In the remainder of this introduction, we review what is known about the social-cognitive skills of human infants and great apes. We look first at young children's understanding of intentional action, then at their understanding of perception and attention, and then at their ability to participate with others in various kinds of shared intentionality involving joint intentions and attention. We then look at these same skills in our nearest primate relatives, especially chimpanzees. We end this introduction by introducing our participants and our methodology for the empirical studies that follow in the four succeeding chapters.

UNDERSTANDING INTENTIONAL ACTION

In the control systems model of Tomasello et al. (in press; based on approaches such as that of Carver & Scheier, 1982), intentional action has three main components—and so understanding intentional actions means understanding something of these three components and their various interrelations. First is the goal. The goal is an internal representation of some state in the environment that the organism desires to be the case. Second is the action. The action is what the organism does, the behavioral means it chooses, in attempting to change the state of the environment in the direction of the goal. This choice is instantiated in an intention to act, which may be more or less "rational" to the degree that it is tailored to meet the particular constraints of current reality. Third is perception. In pursuing its goals, the organism must perceptually monitor the process so as to know when it has and has not successfully achieved its goal—and if at any point it has not it persists in acting, perhaps adjusting its actions "rationally." All of this is hierarchically organized, such that the pursuit of goals in most cases includes setting various kinds of sub-goals and sub-means for pursuing them (e.g., gathering berries requires first getting something to carry them in, then finding them, then picking them, etc.). In some cases, the goal actually encompasses specific means and/or sub-means, as pursuing a goal in a particular way is itself desired. Finally, in some cases the goal may actually be a bodily motion of the organism itself instead of some change of state in the external environment, as, for example, in dancing.

Human infants do not understand all of this, of course. However, there is currently no consensus on precisely when they understand all the various aspects of intentional action and perception. We ourselves fit somewhere in the middle of the current theoretical continuum from "boosters," those who believe that very young infants understand it all (e.g., Trevarthen, 1979) to "scoffers," those who believe that full understanding only comes with the acquisition of language (Carpendale & Lewis, 2004). We are convinced by the convergence of experimental results in many different social-cognitive domains that it is at around their first birthdays that infants begin to understand the basics of the intentional action and perception (see Carpenter, Nagell, & Tomasello, 1998). In terms of explanation, "booster" approaches of course tend to be nativist, assuming that infants' personal experiences

4

play very little role in early social-cognitive development. "Scoffer" approaches mostly derive either from learning theory perspectives, in which social-cognitive development depends on specific learning experiences in specific contexts (e.g., Moore, 1996), or else from a more pragmatist perspectives in which cognition does not reside in mental entities in the head, but rather is imminent in behavior, with a new level of understanding awaiting language (e.g., Carpendale & Lewis, 2004). We ourselves believe that infants come to understand intentional states in others by simulating from their own experience (Tomasello, 1999)—which means that they must first experience in their own case a differentiation of means and ends and so forth (see Sommerville & Woodward, 2005, for evidence)—and they do not do this until the latter part of the first year of life. In any case, we will try to make our case for our interpretation of infants' social-cognitive skills in the remainder of this section, and we will compare our theoretical approach with those of others in more detail in the General Discussion.

Understanding Animate Action

Infants recognize self-produced, biological motion within a few months after birth (Bertenthal, 1996), and by around 6 months of age they have developed sufficient expectations about human animate action to be able to predict what others will do in familiar situations. Thus, for example, using a habituation methodology, Woodward (1998, 1999) found that infants of this age expect people (specifically, human hands) to do such things as reach for objects they were just reaching for previously. Infants do not expect inanimate objects that resemble human hands (e.g., a garden tool "claw") to "reach" toward the familiar object in similar circumstances.

Such studies demonstrate that 6-month-old infants see human actions as animate and object-directed; that is, infants in these studies clearly expect adults to be consistent in their interactions with the same object over a short span of time. But for this infants need only to understand that people spontaneously produce behavior (they are animate beings) and to have some familiarity with what people typically do in familiar circumstances; they do not need to have any understanding of the internal structure of intentional actions. For example, they do not need to know that the actor is evaluating the efficacy of his action toward a goal and persisting in his behavior until he is successful.

Understanding the Pursuit of Goals

By 10 months of age, infants segment streams of continuous behavior into units that correspond to what adults would see as separate goal-directed acts (Baldwin, Baird, Saylor, & Clark, 2001). Infants of this same age also look to an adult's face when the adult teases them with a toy or obstructs their play with a toy (Phillips, Baron-Cohen, & Rutter, 1992; Carpenter, Nagell, & Tomasello, 1998)—perhaps suggesting that infants are seeking information about the adult's goal by trying to discern where the adult is looking or the adult's emotional state. But more than segmenting actions and trying to identify goals, infants of this age also understand an actor's persistence to a goal, that is, they understand that actors perceptually monitor their actions and evaluate their outcomes to determine if and when they match the desired goal state.

The key situations for determining whether infants understand goals as internal representations are situations in which an actor's goal does not match the outcome produced by his action—and the infant should respond in some way to the internal goal and not to the external result. The paradigm cases are failed attempts and accidents. For example, if an adult tries unsuccessfully to give a 9-month-old infant a toy (unsuccessfully because of clumsiness or some obstacle), the infant waits patiently until the adult is successful. In contrast, if the adult simply refuses to give the infant a toy (and the adult's superficial behavior is very similar to that in the situation in which the adult is trying unsuccessfully), infants gesture, reach, bang on the table, and otherwise show their impatience with the adult's unacceptable behavior (Behne, Carpenter, Call, & Tomasello, 2005). They are reacting not to the overt actions or their results—which involve the child not getting a toy in all cases—but to the underlying goal. In habituation studies, infants of this same age also seem to recognize when a computerized dot is adjusting its behavior to an obstacle (Gergeley et al., 1995; Csibra et al., 1999, 2002).

Along these same lines, when slightly older infants (15-month-olds) attempt to imitate adults they do not just mimic the surface behavior, but rather they reproduce the outcome toward which the adults were striving—even if the adults were unsuccessful (Johnson, Booth, & O'Hearn, 2001; Meltzoff, 1995). Infants can tell that adults were unsuccessful in achieving their internally represented goal (it was a failed attempt) when they act on the same object repeatedly, modifying their action each time, which suggests that the outcome of the first act was evaluated as not satisfactory. Similarly, when adults act surprised at the outcome produced by their action ("Whoops!"), infants of this same age very seldom imitate that accidental action, whereas they imitate the action if it is produced in a deliberate manner ("There!"; Carpenter, Akhtar, & Tomasello, 1998). In this case, they can tell that adults were unsuccessful in achieving their goal because the adults' emotional reaction was not one of satisfaction, but rather of surprise.

And so in the months immediately preceding and following their first birthdays, human infants not only know that people are animate agents who direct their actions toward particular objects, they know that they are goal-directed agents who evaluate the outcomes of their actions and persist in acting until they are satisfied that the external result matches their internal goal.

Understanding the Choice of Plans

The most clearly mental aspect of intentional action is the decision-making process by which the actor chooses an action to enact given the reality situation the actor faces. To understand this process, an observer must understand two fundamental things. First, the observer must understand something of the hierarchical structure of intentional action, in the sense that the observer must know that an actor may choose among different lower level plans for effecting some higher level goal. Second, the observer must understand that the actor does not choose among the lower level plans randomly, but rather chooses one for "rational" reasons—in the sense that the actor adjusts its action for the particular reality situation at hand.

Infants seem to understand something of the hierarchical and "rational" structure of intentional action again from around the first birthday. This is suggested by current findings from our laboratory that they sometimes copy the "style" (Hobson & Lee, 1999) with which an adult produces an action toward a goal, even when that style is fairly obviously not causally related to achievement of the goal (Tomasello, Petschauer, & Carpenter (in preparation); see also, e.g., Carpenter, Call, & Tomasello, 2002, and Call, Carpenter, & Tomasello, in press, for studies of this with 2-year-old children). More dramatically, when infants just past their first birthdays observe an adult perform an unusual action for no good reason they, once again, tend to copy it; however, when they see the exact same action performed because of some observable constraint on the actor's behavior (and that constraint is not present for them) they themselves then work toward the goal in the normal, not unusual, way (Gergely, Bekkering, & Király, 2002). Infants thus understand not just that an actor has a goal and a means of action toward that goal, but they also understand something of the reason why the actor chose that particular means to the goal.

To summarize, human infants understand action as animate and object-directed from at least the middle of the first year of life. They understand action as persistent and goal-directed from around 9 months of age, and they manifest this understanding in the most demanding tasks involving imitation from soon after the first birthday. In some cases of imitation, infants of this same age even demonstrate an understanding of some of the reasons why an actor chose a particular means toward a goal in a particular situation. By 14 months of age, then, human infants understand the most fundamental components of intentional action.

An important aspect of this understanding of intentional action is that the observer must understand that the actor perceives the world. This is so that the actor can direct his actions toward the goal objects, avoid obstacles, and, most importantly, evaluate the situation to see if the outcome matches the internally represented goal. Various lines of evidence suggest that infants understand the visual perception of others only gradually, and in a rough parallel to the way they understand the various aspects of intentional action.

Following Gaze

Six-month-old infants follow the gaze direction of adults to very nearby targets (D'Entremont et al., 1997), and 12-month-old infants follow gaze to more distal targets as well (bypassing distractors to do so; Butterworth & Jarrett, 1991). But simple gaze following is not particularly diagnostic in determining how infants understand the visual perception of others, as it may simply reflect a kind of co-orienting mechanism not involving an understanding of the intentional actions or perceptions of the actor at all.

Understanding That Others See Things

Once again at around the first birthday, infants begin to show evidence that they are doing more than simply co-orienting with adults. For example, infants of around 12–14 months of age seem to have some understanding of the mechanisms of perception; for example, they understand the function of the eyes in the looking behavior of others, as they are sensitive to whether adults' eyes are open or closed or blocked by a blindfold when they look in a certain direction (Caron, Butler, & Brooks, 2002; Brooks & Meltzoff, 2002).

Similarly, infants of around this same age do not follow adults' gaze if the adults' line of sight is blocked by some kind of barrier (Butler, Caron, & Brooks, 2000), but they do follow the adult's gaze direction both behind themselves (Flom et al., 2003) and to spaces behind occluding barriers (Moll & Tomasello, 2004). In this latter case, it is noteworthy that infants do more behaviorally than just turn their head in some direction; they actually locomote some distance in order to attain the appropriate viewing angle. Together, these findings suggest at the very least that infants from around their first birthdays understand that other people do not just orient to things but they actually see things.

Understanding That Others Attend to Things

If one views perception not as the passive registering of sensory impressions, but rather in Gibsonian (1966) fashion as the active seeking of information, then perception may be seen as a kind of intentional activity as well. The influence of goals and intentions may be seen most clearly in the process of selective attention—which may be thought of as a kind of intentional perception as the organism chooses to attend to one thing, or one aspect of a thing, based on its current goals (Gibson & Rader, 1979; Tomasello, 1995).

Infants as young as 12–14 months of age show some understanding of selective attention. For example, if an adult looks in the general direction of three objects and becomes very excited, saying something to the infant like "Oh, that's so cool! Can you give it to me?," infants in some situations are able to identify the one object the adult is selectively attending to (based on which one is new in the situation for the adult; Tomasello & Haberl, 2003). Similarly, current findings suggest that if an adult expresses excitement while looking at an object the adult and the infant have just been playing with, the infant assumes the adult is focused on some previously unnoticed aspect of that object or else on some other object (Moll, Koring, Carpenter, & Tomasello, submitted). The social-cognitive skills involved here are thus very similar to those involved in understanding the rational aspects of intentional action, namely, the ability to reason about why actors have chosen to act or to attend in one way rather than another way based on their assessment of the current situation.

Infants' understanding of other people's perception and attention thus develops in tandem with their understanding of intentional action—because perceptual activity is a kind of intentional activity. We might thus say, with some fear of oversimplification, that very young infants understand that animate actors orient to things, at around 9 months infants understand that goal-directed actors see things, and soon after the first birthday infants understand that intentional actors attend to only some of the things they see.

JOINT INTENTIONS AND ATTENTION

Tomasello (1999) assumed that, given a natural primate tendency to interact socially with others, understanding conspecifics as intentional agents who have goals and perceptions would automatically lead to such things as collaboration and joint attentional engagement. But it seems that nonhuman primates also understand many aspects of intentional action and perception, and they nevertheless still do not engage with conspecifics in human-like collaboration and joint attentional engagement (reviewed in the next section). Tomasello et al. (in press) thus proposed that in addition to understanding others as intentional and attentional agents, human beings have evolved special skills and motivations of shared intentionality that enable certain kinds of species-unique social engagement, namely, those that underlie activities involving joint intentions and joint attention.

According to Bratman (1992), joint cooperative activities, as he calls them, have three essential characteristics that distinguish them from social interaction in general (modified slightly here): (1) the interactants are *mutually responsive* to one another; (2) there is a *shared goal* in the sense that each participant has the goal that we (in mutual knowledge) do X together; and (3) the participants coordinate their plans of action and *joint intentions* some way down the hierarchy—which requires that both participants understand and jointly attend to both roles of the interaction (role reversal) and so can at least potentially help the other with his role if needed. Again, the ability to participate in and to understand such activities develops gradually during the infant's first year of life, in parallel with the understanding of intentional action.

Dyadic Engagement: Sharing Behavior and Emotions

Human infants are highly sensitive to social contingencies. In their face-to-face interactions with adults, infants from just a few months of age display the ability to take turns in the sense of acting when the adult is more passive and being more passive when the adult is acting (Trevarthen, 1979). When these contingencies are broken—for example, in experiments in which the adult's behavior is pre-programmed (or played to the infant over delayed video)—infants show various signs of being out of sorts (see Rochat & Striano, 1999; Gergeley & Watson, 1999, for reviews).

But there is another dimension to these interactions that goes beyond simple timing and contingency. Human infants and adults interact with one another dyadically in what are called protoconversations. These are social interactions in which the adult and infant look, touch, smile, and vocalize toward one another in turn-taking sequences. But as most observers of infants have noted, the glue that holds protoconversations together is not just contingency but the exchange of emotions (Trevarthen, 1979; Hobson, 2002). Thus, during protoconversations adult and infant do not just mimic one another or respond randomly, but often express the same emotion using a different behavior (e.g., the adult expresses happiness facially and the child vocally; Stern, 1985). During protoconversations, infants gaze into the eyes of the partner face to face in what is called mutual gazing. It is a dyadic activity in the sense that infants are not monitoring the adult's looking at them or any other object; it is direct engagement.

10

Infants' early social interactions thus clearly show mutual responsiveness, with some degree of what might be called sharing, on the behavioral and emotional levels—perhaps already in ways not shown by other animal species.

Triadic Engagement: Sharing Goals and Perception

Triadic social interactions involving child, adult, and an object of mutual interest begin to occur at around 9–12 months of age, as soon as infants begin to understand that other persons have goals toward objects and see objects. The new kinds of activities are such things as: giving and taking objects, rolling a ball back-and-forth, building a block tower together, putting away toys together, "pretend" games of eating or drinking together, "reading" books together, and pointing-and-naming games (Hay, 1979; Hay & Murray, 1982; Verba, 1994). These activities are triadic from the child's point of view, in the sense that in these activities infants actively monitor the adult's actions and perceptions toward the object of mutual interest and coordinate their own goals and perceptions with those of the adult.

The question from the point of view of shared intentionality is how infants understand their engagement with the adult while participating in these initial triadic activities. So if in building a block tower together the child ignores the adult and simply places blocks on the tower irrespective of what the adult is doing, this is not triadic but individual activity. Or perhaps the child is only responsive to the adult in the sense of taking turns, with no sense of a shared goal. But perhaps adult and child have created a shared goal to build the tower together. This shared goal serves to coordinate their activities around the same object(s) triadically, and thereby to enable each participant to know something about what the other is attending to, and to predict what the other will do next. The interaction is thus more than sharing behavior or emotions dyadically; it is sharing goals and perceptions with respect to some external entity triadically. Although the evidence is less than fully compelling, starting at around 9 months of age infants seem to do a number of things to attempt to re-engage a recalcitrant adult in joint activities—perhaps suggesting a goal to engage in the activity together (shared goal) (Ross & Lollis, 1987; Ratner & Bruner, 1978).

Collaborative Engagement: Joint Intentions and Attention

At around 12–15 months of age, infants' triadic engagements with others undergo a significant qualitative change. Most importantly, it is at this age that infants begin interacting much more in "coordinated joint engagement" in which they coordinate roles with others—even reversing roles with them—in a more active manner (Bakeman & Adamson, 1984).

11

This means, for instance, that the child of this age understands that in pursuing the shared goal of building a block tower the adult holds the edifice steady while the child places blocks; they not only share goals but also formed joint intentions involving coordinated roles. Thus, when in these activities adults stop participating, from about 14 months of age infants not only prompt adults to re-engage, but they sometimes even perform the adults' turn for them (Ross & Lollis, 1987). This might suggest that infants of this age understand not only the shared goal but also the two roles involved, and they are motivated to help adults in their role. Indeed, in situations in which adults do something like hold out a basket (in which the child should place a toy) and then, on the next turn, place the basket in front of the child and hold the toy themselves, some 12- and 18-month-olds take their turn by holding out the basket for the adults and, importantly, looking to them in anticipation of their placing something in it (Carpenter, Tomasello, & Striano, in press). It thus seems that after an initial encounter in one role of an interaction, infants often understand and can perform the other role—an exchanging of roles that may be called role reversal imitation (Tomasello, 1999).

In these interactions, infants are of course also coordinating their perceptions with others in acts of joint attention. An important aspect of these interactions is the infant's comprehension of the adult's communicative intentions, and the infant's own expression of communicative intentions as well—as these overt acts give the participants the possibility not just to follow the others' attention but to direct it as well. In terms of comprehension, infants as young as 14 months of age do more than just follow an adult's point or gaze to a target container in a hiding/finding game; they also (unlike apes) infer that the adult's behavior is for them and therefore relevant to the situation at hand: the adult wanted to inform me that the toy was inside the container toward which he gestured (Behne, Carpenter, & Tomasello, in press). Infants of this age thus understand not just intentions, but communicative intentions.

In terms of production, it is in this same age range that infants make their first nascent attempts to manipulate the attention of others through gestures such as pointing, including declarative pointing in which infants direct adults' attention seemingly for the sole motive of sharing attention. Thus, when an adult reacts to the pointing of a 12-month-old by simply looking to the indicated object, or by looking to the infant (emoting positively), or by doing nothing, infants are not satisfied—implying that these were not their goal. But when the adult responds by looking back and forth from the object to the infant and commenting positively, infants are satisfied—implying that this sharing of attention and interest was their goal (Liszkowski, Carpenter, Henning, Striano, & Tomasello, 2004). Infants of this age will also sometimes point to simply inform adults of things, even though they themselves have no direct interest in them—a kind of helping motive (Liszkowski, Carpenter, Striano, & Tomasello, in press). One-year-olds thus seem to have as goals both joint attention itself and also helping others to attain their goals by directing their attention in relevant ways. And of course language and symbols are not far behind developmentally, and they take both these motives and these skills much further in terms of collaborative activity and role reversal.

By 12–14 months of age, then, the triadic interactions of infants and adults around external entities appear as more "coordinated joint engagement," because the infants can do such things as reverse roles and help adults in their role if needed—both necessary for engaging in joint actions embodying joint intentions. In expressing communicative intentions in gestures and in using linguistic symbols at around this age, infants again demonstrate an understanding of the different but complementary roles in a social interaction as well as a motivation to simply share experience with others and help them toward their goals by informing them of things they want or need to know.

This sharing of psychological states engaged in by human infants and caregivers is internalized and cognitively represented, in Vygotskian fashion, so creating dialogic cognitive representations (Fernyhough, 1996). In these sharing interactions, children understand the adult's psychological states toward things (including themselves and their intentions) at the same time that they experience their own psychological states toward things (including adults and their intentions). This enables children to conceptualize the interaction simultaneously from both a first and third person perspective (see Barresi & Moore, 1996) and so form a "bird's eye view" of the collaboration in which all components are within a single representational format—which constitutes a dialogic cognitive representation. During months and even years of such interactions, from ages 1 to 5 and beyond, children come to construct in dialogic fashion representations of such things as social norms and their constitutive conventional practices and individual beliefs.

Ontogenetic Patterns

An obvious question at this point is how these many different social-cognitive skills relate to one another during ontogeny. When infants are tested regularly from 9 to 15 months of age on a battery of tasks, the earliest skills have to do with sharing with others, specifically in the form of engaging with them in joint attentional interactions and holding up things to show them to others (Carpenter, Nagell, & Tomasello, 1998). Skills of following attention (e.g., gaze following to distant targets) and directing attention to distant targets (e.g., distal pointing) come only later. It is also true

13

that all of these skills emerge together in close developmental synchrony for individual infants (typically within a 4-month window) in an intercorrelated manner. This developmental pattern is consistent with the view of early social-cognitive development as the interaction of two strands of development—the general primate line of understanding others as goal-directed agents and the uniquely human line of sharing psychological states with others—with the uniquely human, sharing, line actually beginning to emerge first.

In the case of nonhuman primates—who, by hypothesis, do not possess the sharing line of development—we would thus expect to see a human-like understanding of intentional action and perception fairly early in development but no forms of shared intentionality at any point in development.

THE SOCIAL COGNITION OF GREAT APES

The nature of great apes' social-cognitive skills is currently the subject of much debate. The fundamental question is what the researcher accepts as evidence. Thus, some theorists believe that as apes are so close to us phylogenetically, simply observing them behaving—preferably in their natural environments but in other environments as well—is sufficient to infer the underlying cognitive processes involved. Thus, Boesch and Boesch-Achermann (2000) attribute many social-cognitive skills to chimpanzees based on the way they interact socially in their natural environment; de Waal (1982) makes similar attributions based on chimpanzees "political" interactions in captive settings; and Savage-Rumbaugh et al. (1998) argue that the best way to understand chimpanzee social cognition is for the researcher to interact with them directly on a long-term basis (participant observation). In general, researchers who privilege observations of this type believe that chimpanzees' social-cognitive skills are very similar to those of humans (and they typically provide no specific hypotheses about how the two species might differ, or how apes might differ from other animal species, whom many other observers—both scientific and lay—believe have sophisticated cognitive skills as well). On the opposite side of things, some theorists do not believe that chimpanzees have any social-cognitive skills at all beyond the ability to observe and predict the overt behavior of others based on learned stimulus-response contingencies. Thus, Povinelli and Vonk (2003) not only dismiss inferences to social-cognitive skills based on natural observations, they also believe that experiments—which are essentially controlled observations—are also insufficient to infer underlying cognitive processes.

The middle position, and the one to which we subscribe, is that cognitive and social-cognitive process can be inferred on the basis of observation—to deny this is to deny the utility of almost all of cognitive and cognitive-developmental psychology—but natural observations are normally only suggestive because they most often leave open too many interpretive possibilities. For example, if an individual primate is being chased by another and stops to look for a predator, which distracts the chaser, was the chasee attempting to deceive the chaser (create a false belief)? To establish this, we need to know—at the very least and among other things—how often individuals stop to look for predators when they are *not* being chased, which could be established either by control observations or perhaps in an experiment. And so while natural observations are invaluable for generating hypotheses, we subscribe to the view that the systematic observations made in experiments—in which behavior is observed systematically under different conditions which the researcher controls—are the most important kinds of observations for inferring underlying cognitive and social-cognitive processes.

Taking this middle way, in which all observations are relevant but experimental observations are considered most reliable, Tomasello and Call (1997) reviewed all of the available evidence and concluded that nonhuman primates understand much about the behavior of conspecifics but nothing about their intentions or other psychological states. The few experiments that existed at this time gave mostly negative results, or else had methodological flaws that enabled other plausible interpretations (e.g., the well-known study of Premack & Woodruff, 1978). In the last few years, however, new data have emerged suggesting that at least some nonhuman primates—the research is mainly with chimpanzees[1]—do understand at least some psychological states, such as goals and perceptions, in others. At the moment it is still unclear, however, the degree to which these skills are similar to those of human children (many task variations have not been carried out with nonhuman primates), and whether nonhuman primates have either the ability or the motivation to share psychological states with others in acts of shared intentionality involving joint intentions and attention. We also know almost nothing about the ontogeny of these social-cognitive skills in apes, and the ways in which the process is similar to and different from the human version (Parker & McKinney, 1999, p. 147).

Understanding Intentional Action

Nonhuman primates are clearly able to use a variety of cues to predict the behavior of others in familiar situations. For example, tamarin monkeys expect that people continue to reach for an object that they have previously gazed at, just like human infants (Santos & Hauser, 1999), and chimpanzees, also like human infants, expect animated dots on a computer screen to continue to pursue the same external goal even if this involves using a different spatial trajectory (Uller, 2004).

There is even some evidence that apes understand both failed attempts and accidents, in which the desired result never happens—which, as argued above, are especially diagnostic in determining if an organism understands goals as internal representations. Thus, when a human gives food to an ape repeatedly, but then suddenly refuses, the ape shows impatience (gestures, bangs, leaves); but when the human makes good faith but unsuccessful attempts the ape waits (relatively) patiently—just as the human infants did in the study of Behne et al. (2005) (Call, Hare, Carpenter, & Tomasello, 2004). Chimpanzees thus apparently can understand the frustrating behavior of humans sometimes as persistent attempts (trying) to give them food. With regard to accidents, chimpanzees also wait (relatively) patiently when the human makes a good faith, but clumsy and unsuccessful, effort to give them food (Call et al. (2004); see also Call and Tomasello (1998), for further evidence that chimpanzees and orangutans distinguish between purposeful and accidental actions.)

Although nonhuman primates are not very good imitators—they tend to reproduce the result in the environment (emulation learning) and pay very little attention to the actual actions of the demonstrator (see Call & Carpenter, 2003; Tomasello, 1996a, for reviews)—there is some weak evidence that chimpanzees, like children, will perform a target action (in terms of the end result produced) equally as often when they see a failed attempt as when they see the completed action (Call, Carpenter, & Tomasello, in press; Myowa-Yamakoshi & Matsuzawa, 2000). There are no imitation studies looking at apes' understanding of accidents, nor are there any studies investigating their ability to reproduce the pure style of the actor's action or to understand the rationality underlying an actor's choice of a particular means of action. Such studies might be especially feasible with apes raised by humans, as they are more likely to engage in something resembling humanlike imitative learning (Tomasello, Savage-Rumbaugh, & Kruger, 1993; Call & Tomasello, 1996).

Understanding Perception and Attention

Chimpanzees clearly understand that others see things. First of all, they follow conspecific gaze direction to external targets (Tomasello, Call, & Hare, 1998), and current results from our laboratory suggest that they even follow gaze direction when all they see is the back of the looker's head (Tomasello, Lehmann, Hare, & Call, in preparation). In addition, if apes follow human gaze and see nothing there, they check back with the looker, much as human infants do (Call et al., 1998). If they keep following an individual's gaze and finding nothing there, they soon quit looking (Tomasello, Hare, & Fogleman, 2001). And when a human looks to a target behind a barrier, chimpanzees will locomote some distance in order to fixate the same target (Tomasello, Hare, & Agnetta, 1999). Great apes thus follow the gaze direction of others in a very flexible manner, suggesting an understanding that others see particular targets. Chimpanzees also know that what others see affects what they do. Thus, when a dominant and a subordinate individual compete with one another over food—with some pieces of food visible to both individuals and some visible only to the subordinate individual—subordinates most often pursue the piece of food hidden from the dominant's view (Hare et al., 2000, 2001), thus demonstrating that they know that the dominant will go for the food it can see. Relatedly, in a competitive situation chimpanzees go to some lengths to conceal their own approach to contested food from their competitor (Hare et al., in press).

Chimpanzees also understand a good bit about the mechanisms of visual perception. For example, they only produce visually based gestures when their potential recipient is facing them (Tomasello et al., 1994, 1997). Although not performing skillfully in some experimental situations (Povinelli & Eddy, 1996), when chimpanzees are faced with a single human experimenter in different orientations (e.g., back turned, back turned but looking over the shoulder to the ape, facing the ape but head looking away, facing the ape but eyes closed), they mostly gesture appropriately, depending on whether the human is in a position to see their gesture and/or give them food (Kaminski, Call, & Tomasello, 2004). Apes do not seem to gesture differently, however, in the situation in which a human is facing them with eyes open and one in which the human is facing them with eyes closed.

And so apes almost certainly understand that others see things, although it is not clear that they understand the role of the eyes specifically in this process. There are no studies that assess whether apes understand attention as a selective process in which the perceiver makes active choices about what to pay attention to, and none of these skills have been investigated specifically with apes raised in close contact with humans, who might be expected to pay more attention to the visual experience of others.

Joint Intentions and Attention

Despite this sophistication in understanding many important aspects of intentional action and perception, apes still seem to lack the motivations and skills for even the most basic forms of shared intentionality. Thus, while ape infants interact with their mothers dyadically and are responsive to them behaviorally (Maestripieri & Call, 1994) and they may even show some maternal gazing and social smiling (Mizuno & Takeshita, 2002; Tomonaga et al., 2004), there are no observations of anything like protoconversations between adults and infants or otherwise sharing psychological states with one another. Although all primates display similar social emotions in terms of attachment between babies and mothers, human infants and mothers seem to possess a much larger behavioral repertoire for expressing a much wider range of emotions in their social interactions than do other apes—especially expressions of positive emotion serving to enrich the dyadic emotional engagement between mother and child (e.g., laughing, cooing, smiling).

Further along this line, apes engage in very few triadic interactions with others around objects. They beg food from one another, and youngsters' play sometimes incorporates objects. But systematic observations of ape mothers and infants with objects reveal very little triadic engagement, and none that appears to involve a shared goal (Bard & Vauclair, 1984; Tomonaga et al., 2004). When apes interact with humans, they engage in more triadic interactions, but these interactions are still discernibly different from those of human mothers and children. For example, when interacting with an adult human, human children spend far more time in episodes of alternating attention (about double) than do apes, and their looks to the face of the adult are, on average, almost twice as long as those of the apes (Carpenter, Tomasello, & Savage-Rumbaugh, 1995). Children's looks to the adult are also sometimes accompanied by smiles, whereas apes do not smile in triadic situations—giving the impression that the ape's look to the adult is a checking look (to see what the adult is doing or is likely to do next), whereas the child's look to the adult is a sharing look (to share interest). One interpretation of this pattern of observations is that although apes know that others have goals and perceptions, they have little desire to share them. They can interact with others triadically around objects, but they do not engage with others in joint actions with shared goals and experiences.

In their natural environment, chimpanzees join one another in agonistic interactions within the group (so-called coalitions and alliances), and they act together to defend the group from predators and other chimpanzee groups. But in these interactions, each individual does basically the same thing, and they do it without coordinated plans. The most complex cooperative activity of chimpanzees is group hunting, in which two or more males seem to play different roles in corralling a monkey (Boesch & Boesch, 1989). But in analyses of the sequential unfolding of participant behavior over time in these hunts, many observers have characterized this activity as essentially identical to the group hunting of other social mammals such as lions and wolves (Cheney & Seyfarth, 1990; Tomasello & Call, 1997). Although it is a complex social activity, as it develops over time each individual simply assesses the state of the chase at each moment and decides what is best for it to do. There is nothing that would be called collaboration in the narrow sense of joint intentions and attention based on coordinated plans. In experimental studies (e.g., Crawford, 1937; Chalmeau, 1994), the most complex behavior so far demonstrated is two chimpanzees pulling a heavy object in parallel, and during this activity almost no spontaneous communication among partners is observed (Povinelli & O'Neill, 2000). There are no published experimental studies in which chimpanzees collaborate by playing different and complementary roles in an activity. Again it seems that apes and other nonhuman primates do not formulate with one another shared goals or joint plans and intentions.

Similarly, ape communication also does not seem to be about sharing experience in the same way as does much of human communication. Most basically, there is very little communication about third entities (topics), and there are no signals expressing a declarative or informative motive.[2] Apes do not point, show, or even actively offer things to conspecifics, and their gestural signals are not really bidirectional in the sense that sender and receiver both know that either could play either role (i.e., they do not know it is the same signal when they send it as when they receive it).[3] There are also a number of experimental studies demonstrating that apes are not able to understand communicative intentions as manifest in such acts as a human pointing or placing a marker to indicate the location of food (see Call & Tomasello, in press, for a review).

The overall conclusion would thus seem to be that although apes interact with one another in myriad complex ways, they are not motivated in the same way as humans to share emotions, experiences, and activities with others of their own kind. They do not look to others and smile in order to share experience triadically, they do not invite others to share interest and attention via declarative gestures, they do not inform others of things (share information) or help them in their efforts, and they do not engage with others in collaborative activities with shared goals and joint intentions. But what if they are raised in a human cultural environment in which they are encouraged to engage in collaborative activities and communicate with symbols? Savage-Rumbaugh (1990) reports that the bonobo Kanzi participates regularly in social activities such as preparing food and playing with toys. But it is not clear if he has the kind of commitment to these activities as joint endeavors that characterizes human collaboration, nor is it clear that he understands the role of the other or supports the other in it. In his mainly imperative attempts at communication, Kanzi does not seem to be motivated to simply share interest with or inform others (Greenfield & Savage-Rumbaugh, 1991). But, in general, the basic fact is that neither Kanzi nor other human-raised apes have participated in the kinds of diagnostic experimental paradigms needed to determine these things.

It should also be noted that we know very little about the ontogeny of any of these skills in developing apes—understanding intentions, understanding attention, or acting with joint intentions and attention—and virtually nothing about their interrelations in ontogeny (i.e., there is nothing

19

comparable with the infant longitudinal study of Carpenter, Nagell, & Tomasello, 1998, carried out with apes).

PLAN OF THE *MONOGRAPH*

In the current *Monograph*, we investigate the social-cognitive development of three young chimpanzees using tasks that have previously been used with human infants, mainly in the 1–2-year age range. We therefore rely on the logic of the comparative method in which traits that are common to two or more species are attributed to their common ancestor, whereas traits that differ are attributed to their subsequent individual evolutions. The method of comparison is well established in evolutionary biology in general, for example, for anatomical traits, but when applied to behavior and cognition it is not without controversy.

The Comparative Method

In the middle part of the 20th century, behaviorists were interested in comparing a wide variety of species on various learning tasks. For example, Bitterman (1965) compared several extant species of insect, fish, and mammal on such things as speed to learn a simple perceptual discrimination, speed to learn a reversal of contingencies, and other learning skills. An implicit assumption of much of this work was that just as morphology became ever more complex from insect to fish to mammals to humans, so behavior should show this same "progression." But Comparative Psychology came under attack from its inception by researchers who felt that studying such different animal species on experimental tasks for which they were not naturally adapted was a misguided enterprise (e.g., Beach, 1950; Hodos & Campbell, 1969). They charged that studies such as Bitterman's smacked of a scala naturae in which some animals were "higher" or "more intelligent" than others, with, of course, humans atop the heap. That is, many of the comparative studies of learning implicitly assumed that non-human animals represented primitive steps on the way to humans as evolutionary telos. This contradicted the established Darwinian fact of tree-like branching evolution in which no living species was a primitive version of any other living species, but rather each extant species was its own telos.

Today, therefore, modern comparative studies typically compare only species that are fairly closely related to one another phylogentically—thus ensuring at least some commonalties of ecology and adaptation based on their relatively short times as distinct species—and these comparisons are made on the basis of some clear theoretical rationale. In the current studies, we adopt this more modern approach by comparing two closely related

20

species—humans and chimpanzees—using tasks directly relevant to a theory of human evolutionary uniqueness. The tasks in the current study were therefore chosen from among many already conducted with human infants, for reasons of theoretical relevance, and they were then adapted for young chimpanzees so as to fit with their natural proclivities (e.g., of attention and manipulation and motivation) as much as possible. In addition, it is also important that the chimpanzee individuals in the current study were raised by humans from birth and were tested by humans with whom they were very familiar—thus ensuring that the testing situation was something very natural in the lives of these particular individuals.

The Participants

The main participants in the study were three young chimpanzees: Alexandra, Annet, and Alex (see Figure 1). Alexandra and Annet were young female chimpanzees of the West African variety (*Pan troglodytes verus*). They were both born in the same medical research facility in August of 1999. Because both were rejected by their natural mothers, they were raised from birth by humans with bottle-feeding and other human care. Gradually, they began spending the better part of their day in a group of five orphan chimpanzees of about the same age. During this time, their interaction with humans was centered mainly around care-giving activities. In June of 2001, when they were around 22 months of age, they came to the Wolfgang Köhler Primate Research Center, where they were cared for by a staff of human caretakers. For the first year or so, their interactions with humans in their new home continued to center around care-giving activities. After that, there was more interaction with humans around toys and other human artifacts for some months (although this was never systematic), during which time most of the testing took place.

Alex was a young male chimpanzee (sub-species unknown) born in March of 2001 who was rejected by his mother at birth in a zoo in France. He was raised in a human home for the first year of his life, with continuous interaction with humans in all kinds of human activities (i.e., he was treated much like a human child). In May of 2002, at around 14 months of age he came to the Wolfgang Köhler Primate Research Center, where he continued to receive this same kind of rich interaction with humans and their artifacts on a daily basis. Normally, he participated in this kind of activity for around 6 hours per day.

A fourth baby chimpanzee, Mosi (male, *P. troglodytes verus*), came to the Wolfgang Köhler Primate Research Center soon after birth, also because he was rejected by his mother at birth. He received human care from birth, but died at around 9 months of age. He was tested several times in the lon-

(a)

[Photo by Daniela Rogge]

(b)

[Photo by Mike Seres]

FIGURE 1.—The participants: (a) from left to right, Alexandra, Annet, and Alex; (b) Mosi.

gitudinal study, and these data are reported below; he participated in none of the experiments, which were conducted at older ages.

In each of the experimental studies reported in Chapters 3, 4, and 5, only Alexandra, Annet, and Alex participated. For each of these studies, the age(s) at which each chimpanzee participated are reported in Table 1. In the longitudinal study reported in Chapter 2, all four chimpanzees participated (although Mosi did so only for 4 months). For this study, the ages at which each chimpanzee participated are reported in Figure 3. Except when otherwise noted, the experimenters were familiar caregivers who had spent much time with the chimpanzees in their everyday lives, and so could go into the enclosure with them. All sessions were videotaped.

As more general information about the species, chimpanzees are one of two species of the genus *Pan* (the other being bonobos, *Pan paniscus*) which shared a common ancestor with humans approximately 6 million years ago—with the two species of *Pan* splitting about 2 million years ago. Chimpanzees live naturally throughout equatorial Africa, inhabiting both trees and ground at different periods of the day, surviving mainly on fruit and other vegetation (but supplementing this with insects and some meat). They live in so-called "fission–fusion" societies in which small bands of several individuals forage together for part of the day, with band composition changing relatively often and the majority of individuals coming together to sleep at the end of the day (Goodall, 1986).

In terms of early ontogeny, chimpanzees reach all of the major motor milestones of infancy many months before human infants. Their brains, which as adults are in the end about one-third the size of humans', also develop at a faster rate than those of human infants. There are very few systematic cognitive-developmental data, but on such tasks as object permanence and tool use chimpanzees develop at very similar rates to human infants (Chevalier-Skolnikoff, 1977, 1989), although they may reach Stage 6 of Piagetian sensory-motor development a bit later (Antinucci, 1989). Socially, chimpanzee infants stay in very close contact with their mothers for the first few years of life, leaving physical contact mostly to play with other infants (or sometimes adults) for ever longer periods of time, starting sometime after the first birthday (with fairly large individual differences; Goodall, 1986; Plooij, 1984). Chimpanzee infants are responsive to human faces from soon after birth, and their behavioral profile in standardized assessments such as the Brazelton Neonatal Assessment Inventory (given soon after birth) is not so different from that of human infants (Bard, Platzman, Lester, & Suomi, 1992). Recent studies show that chimpanzees engage in neonatal imitation in much the same way as human infants (Myowa, 1996; Myowa-Yamakoshi, Tomonaga, Tanaka, & Matsusawa, 2004), and they follow gaze direction to very near targets from early in development in much the same way as human infants (Okamoto et al., 2002)—in both cases with a human demonstrator. Raising chimpanzees in the midst of humans and their cultural artifacts (including language) can lead them to adopt some more human-like patterns of social behavior and cognition than

23

TABLE 1

The Age(s) at Which Each Subject Participated in Each of the Experimental Studies in Chapters 3–5

	Age (Months)														
	16	17	28	35	36	37	38	40	41	45	47	53	55	59	63
Alex	ACC1, STY1, STY2	STY3	ACC2	FA, RR		BAR, MEC, ATT1		CI	RAT, ATT2	ATT3					
Alexandra				STY1	ACC1, STY2		STY3				ACC2, MEC	FA, RR	BAR, ATT1	RAT, ATT2, CI	ATT3
Annet				STY1	ACC1, STY2		STY3				ACC2, MEC	FA, RR	BAR, ATT1	RAT, ATT2, CI	ATT3

FA, failed attempts; ACC, accidents; STY, copy style; RAT, rational plans; BAR, following gaze around barriers; MEC, mechanisms of perception; ATT, understanding attention; RR, role reversal; CI, understanding communicative intentions.

is typical of their wild conspecifics (Hayes, 1952; Kellogg & Kellogg, 1933; Ladygina-Kohts, 2002; Gardner, Gardner, & van Cantfort, 1989; Savage-Rumbaugh & Lewin, 1994), especially with regard to imitation and some gestures (see Call & Tomasello, 1996, for a review).

The Studies

The three chimpanzees were tested in (a) a battery of tasks in a series of longitudinal assessments and (b) nine experimental protocols complete with control conditions.

LONGITUDINAL ASSESSMENTS

All three of the young chimpanzees were assessed longitudinally over time on a battery of social-cognitive tasks (and a few nonsocial cognitive tasks to act as controls), with the fourth chimpanzee, Mosi, tested only from 5–8 months of age. This battery and the procedures involved were based very closely on those of the Carpenter, Nagell, and Tomasello (1998) study of human infants. We tested the following skills:

Attention following
  Gaze following
  Point following

Behavior following (imitation)
  Instrumental actions
  Arbitrary actions

Communicative gestures
  Proximal declaratives (mainly showing)
  Distal declaratives (mainly pointing)
  Imperatives

Joint attention
  Triadic joint engagement

Obstacle tasks
  Social obstacle
  Physical obstacle

Object-related tasks
  Object permanence
  Spatial relations

25

The main difference with the Carpenter, Nagell, and Tomasello (1998) study was that the chimpanzees, especially Alexandra and Annet, were at somewhat older ages than the infants when this longitudinal study took place.

EXPERIMENTAL ASSESSMENTS

In terms of the experiments, four of the nine tasks had to do with the understanding of intentional action as expressed in imitative responses of one kind or another:
Understanding intentional action

  (1) Failed attempts (after Meltzoff, 1995);
  (2) accidents (after Carpenter, Akhtar, & Tomasello, 1998);
  (3) copying style (after Hobson & Lee, 1999; Tomasello et al., submitted);
  (4) rational plans (after Gergely et al., 2002).

Another three of these experimental protocols had to do with the understanding of perception and attention:
Understanding perception and attention

  (1) Following gaze around barriers (after Moll & Tomasello, 2004);
  (2) mechanisms of perception (after Kaminski et al., 2004);
  (3) understanding attention (after Moll et al., submitted).

Finally, two of the experimental protocols had to do with the forming of joint intentions and attention:
Joint intentions and attention

  (1) Collaboration with role reversal (after Carpenter et al., in press);
  (2) understanding communicative intentions (after Behne, Carpenter, & Tomasello, in press).

The specifics of the task protocols will be given below as each experiment is reported.

The Hypotheses

Based on the theoretical proposals of Tomasello et al. (in press) and on previous findings, we hypothesized that the young chimpanzees would show human-like skills in all of the experiments and tests that concerned a basic understanding of the goal-directed action and perception of others, including: failed attempts, accidents, following gaze around barriers, and mechanisms of perception—as well as the longitudinal tasks of this same type. We predicted that they would *not* show human-like skills in tests that required something in the direction of joint intentions and attention (shared intentionality), including: collaboration/role reversal, understanding communicative intentions, and the longitudinal tasks having to do with joint attention and the production of declarative gestures.

In the longitudinal study specifically, our expectation was that the absence of skills involving shared intentionality would lead to some ontogenetic patterns different from those observed in typically developing human infants. However, beyond the absence of skills of shared intentionality, it was unclear what to expect about the specific ontogenetic sequences we might observe in our developing chimpanzee youngsters. One possibility was that in the other skills that do not involve shared intentionality, chimpanzees might show the same pattern of following before directing attention and behavior, like children with autism when tested with the same battery (Carpenter, Pennington, & Rogers, 2002).

There were three experimental tasks for which no predictions were made. First, in previous research apes have not shown much skill at copying the specific behaviors of others, and so we might expect them to do poorly in the copy style experiment. However, apes raised and/or trained by humans sometimes seem to pay more attention to human behavior (Custance, Whiten, & Bard, 1995; Call, 2001), so it was possible that the chimpanzees in the current study would do some of this. Second, there were no clear expectations for the rational plans experiment. Although chimpanzees apparently understand something about others' goals, there are as yet no studies of their understanding that others form intentions rationally. Third, there were no clear expectations in the attention experiment, which required youngsters to discern where an excited human's attention was focused based on an understanding of what was old and new information for her. Again, although chimpanzees apparently understand something about others' perception, there are no studies of their understanding of attention, in the sense of deliberately focusing on one or another aspect of the environment.

It should be highlighted at the beginning that with only three subjects our analytical options were limited. Our general approach, where it was possible, was to administer multiple trials of the same task—using different materials to minimize practice effects (and sometimes with significant lags of time)—and thereby, hopefully, to obtain a more reliable estimate of a particular individual's skills. The same orders and counterbalancing were used for each subject in most cases in order to better be able to compare results across subjects. Our general analytic procedure was as follows:

- we present data for each individual in each analysis for each study, so that readers can have access to something close to the raw data;

- in cases where we can do statistical analyses on individuals (because we have sufficient numbers of trials) we do that, and then draw conclusions about that individual—with summary statements about the pattern across the three individuals;
- in cases where we cannot analyze individuals statistically, we simply note whether the distributions between the different experimental conditions "segregate" (i.e., all of the scores in one condition are higher than even the highest score of the other condition) or overlap;
- in cases where the distributions segregate we present a group test statistic, with $n = 3$, typically a simple t-test—which obviously must be taken with great caution.

NOTES

1. Of the 200+ species of nonhuman primates, systematic research has been done with only a few. Here and throughout we refer either to "nonhuman primates," when we have no reason to believe that any primate species differ, or to "great apes" when there is evidence that at least some great apes show a skill but other nonhuman primate species do not (or vice versa).

2. Vervet monkey alarm calls and the like do not need to be interpreted as informing others, and indeed individuals have very little control over their production at all (Owren & Rendall, 2001). Moreover, there is no evidence that any ape species uses such calls.

3. Although sometimes presented in this way, the study of Povinelli, Nelson, and Boysen (1990) has other interpretations not involving role reversal (Tomasello & Call, 1997).

II. THE EMERGENCE OF SOCIAL COGNITION: A LONGITUDINAL STUDY

During the early ontogeny of our three chimpanzee subjects, we administered a battery of social-cognitive tasks longitudinally—based as closely as possible on those of Carpenter, Nagell, and Tomasello (1998, Study 1) with 9–15-month-old human infants. These tasks were administered in controlled ways, but in the context of natural play and interaction and with more than one task variation where possible—to do everything possible to detect competence in a task at the youngest age possible. The multiple administrations over time were designed to reveal any developmental relations among basic social-cognitive abilities in early chimpanzee ontogeny, and they also gave us our best chance to detect evidence that chimpanzees can engage in some kinds of very basic collaborative or sharing activities such as sharing attention either by interacting with the human in some kind of joint engagement with an object or by gesturing to the human declaratively to simply share attention. Our two main goals in this study were:

(1) To investigate the developmental relations among four basic social-cognitive skills that are important in early human development: responding appropriately to adult points and gaze (attention following); imitating instrumental and arbitrary acts (behavior following); communicative gestures (declarative: attention directing; imperative: behavior directing); and joint engagement.

(2) To provide more facilitative opportunities for the young chimpanzees to show evidence of joint intentionality by interacting with the adult and an object in some kind of joint engagement and/or by gesturing for the human declaratively.

Because the study was modeled on that of Carpenter, Nagell, and Tomasello (1998), we can compare our results both to those of typically developing children from that study and to those of young children with

29

autism, who were administered this same battery by Carpenter, Pennington, and Rogers (2002).

Carpenter, Nagell, and Tomasello (1998) tested five social-cognitive skills longitudinally at monthly intervals between 9 and 15 months of age: joint engagement, communicative gestures, attention following, imitative learning, and referential language (with multiple task variations of each). All of the skills were predicted to emerge together, as they were all thought to involve a coherent and emerging understanding of other persons as intentional and attentional agents who had both goals/intentions and perception/ attention. Evidence consistent with this hypothesis was found, as all of the skills emerged together for most children within a short time window from 9 to 12 months of age, they did so in a reliable order, and there were correlations among ages of emergence of each of the main skills (whereas few such correlations were found with object-related skills that did not involve any social-cognitive skills).

The same developmental pattern of emergence of the various social-cognitive skills was observed in the majority of infants. First, infants *shared attention* with adults in joint engagement (and shortly thereafter, they shared attention somewhat more actively by declaratively showing objects to others). Then, infants *followed others' attention* by looking where they looked or pointed. Then, infants *followed others' behavior* by imitating their actions on objects. Finally, infants *directed others' attention* and then *directed others' behavior* through the use of distal declarative and imperative gestures such as pointing.

Carpenter et al. (2002) tested young children with autism on this same task battery, although only at a single visit. They found that for most children with autism, unlike other children, tests involving others' attention were more difficult than tests involving others' behavior. However, within the domains of attention and behavior, the typical pattern of sharing, then following, and then directing was evident. Turner, Pozdol, Ulman, and Stone (2003) have recently replicated these basic findings with younger children with autism who were followed longitudinally.

There are no studies that systematically investigate the development of these social-cognitive skills in any nonhuman primate longitudinally—and none, to our knowledge, that administer a battery of these types of social-cognitive tasks to the same individuals. As noted in the introduction, Bard and Vauclair (1984) systematically observed some ape mothers and infants interacting with objects, Carpenter et al. (1995) observed some apes in interaction with humans with special attention to skills of joint attentional engagement and Tomonaga et al. (2004) observed for joint engagement, gaze and point following, and some communicative gestures. None of these studies revealed strong evidence for skills of collaborative or joint attentional engagement (although each used different methods and scoring criteria than the current study), or for any kind of declarative gesturing. The hope in our case was that repeated administrations over developmental time, with several variations of each task, would reveal some skills in this domain not revealed by those two studies.

METHOD

Participants

Participants were all four chimpanzees. Mosi was tested four times (from age 5 through 8 months), Alex was tested eight times (from age 15 through 30 months), and Annet and Alexandra were tested five times each (from age 26 through 48 months); see the white cells in Figure 3, for details about the exact ages at which chimpanzees were tested.

Procedure

Chimpanzees were tested in a familiar room (their indoor living area) by a familiar caretaker (E) and with another familiar caretaker (E2) present and sitting with them on the floor (see Figure 2). This second caretaker helped keep the chimpanzees focused on the task at hand by, for example, holding them back during demonstrations (as was done in the human infant study). Tasks were not administered in any way outside the testing sessions and the E's did not assist chimpanzees in any way during testing. Also present at testing were two other familiar humans for scoring and filming, who stayed in the background and did not interact with the chimpanzees. Three video cameras deployed in different corners of the room (integrated through a quad-splitter) were used in an attempt to capture anything relevant that chimpanzees did.

The procedure from Carpenter, Nagell, and Tomasello's (1998) Study 1 was used, with the only exception that some of the toys used were different from those used by children, but every effort was made to ensure that they were similar types of toys. Otherwise, the procedures and the criteria for passing were identical in the two studies. The series of tests was administered in a predetermined, random order, with four different sets of objects alternating across visits to limit practice effects. If on any administration of any test, the E's agreed that the chimpanzee was not attending appropriately, that trial was discounted and re-administered either immediately or at the end of the session. The basics of the tests are described below; see Carpenter, Nagell, and Tomasello (1998) for more details. Each testing session lasted between 1 and 2 hours, with breaks during it as needed.

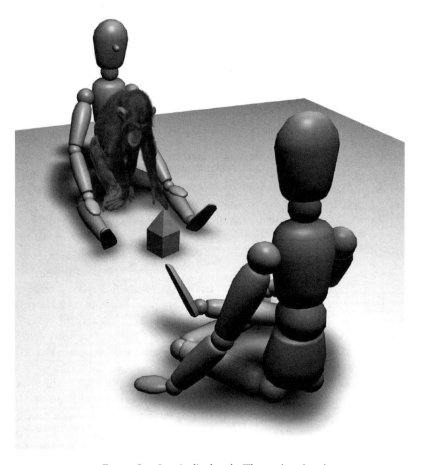

FIGURE 2.—*Longitudinal study*: The testing situation.

Sharing Attention

Joint Engagement

Videotapes of the entire testing session at each visit were coded for joint engagement with E or E2. Joint engagement was scored when chimpanzees spontaneously looked from an object to the adult's face and back to the same object in a coordinated way (objects included the many, various toys played with during and between the tests). Chimpanzees passed this skill if they initiated at least one such episode.

Following Attention and Behavior

Attention Following

For *gaze following* tests, E called the chimpanzee by name, waited for eye contact, and then with an excited facial expression and vocalization (a gasp) alternated her gaze (turning her head) between the chimpanzee's eyes and the assigned target (one of four stuffed animals) several times. The procedure for *point following* tests was identical with the addition that E pointed to the target. Chimpanzees passed gaze and point following if they correctly localized the target on each of two trials (one on the left and one on the right). They passed attention following if they passed either gaze or point following.

Imitative Learning

Boxes like those of Carpenter, Nagell, and Tomasello (1998) were used (similar to those depicted in Figure 8). For imitative learning of *instrumental actions*, there were two attachments on the top of the 30 × 30 × 15 cm box, for example, a doorstop and a spring, with the target action being "lifting the doorstop." For imitative learning of *arbitrary actions*, there were no attachments on the 30 × 46 × 16 cm box; target actions included such things as bending down at the waist and touching one's forehead to the top of the box, rubbing the top of the box, or kicking the top of the box. Each time the target action was performed, some interesting result at the back of the box happened, for example, a set of colored lights lit up. After a 1–2 minutes baseline period during which chimpanzees were encouraged to play with the box, E modeled the target action (or if chimpanzees had spontaneously performed the target action in the baseline period, E modeled an alternate action, replacing the attachment if necessary) three times and then encouraged chimpanzees to take a turn. Chimpanzees were given approximately 1 minute to respond, and then this sequence of model and response was repeated. In order to determine whether chimpanzees were reproducing E's action with the same goal (i.e., turning on the lights), the lights were delayed by 1 second during response periods and we coded whether chimpanzees looked in anticipation to the lights. Chimpanzees passed an imitative learning test whether they reproduced or attempted to reproduce the modeled action with an expectant look to the lights. They passed imitative learning if they passed either the imitation of instrumental actions or the imitation of arbitrary actions test.

Directing Attention and Behavior

Communicative Gestures

Four situations, similar to those used by Mundy, Sigman, Ungerer, and Sherman (1987) were presented in an attempt to elicit production of gestures. To elicit declarative gestures, two unusual events occurred (a stuffed animal began to dance in mid-air and a puppet appeared and moved around at the door) and the adults pretended not to notice. To elicit imperative gestures, an attractive toy was placed in a locked, transparent box and a wind-up toy was stopped. Following Perucchini and Camaioni (1993), adults first reacted to any chimpanzee gestures or repeated gaze alternation to E and the object by alternating gaze between the object and the chimpanzee with an excited reaction (e.g., "Oh, yes, look at that!"). After any further gesturing, E helped the chimpanzee with the imperative toys. This two-step response by the adults was designed to help identify whether chimpanzee gestures were imperative or declarative. If chimpanzees continued gesturing after the adult's sharing response, this indicated that chimpanzees were not satisfied with this response and wanted something else from the adult, so they were coded as imperatives (whereas if they stopped gesturing after E's response they were coded as declaratives). Spontaneous productions of intentionally communicative gestures (i.e., that were accompanied by gaze alternation between the object and any adult's face) were coded during these situations as well as during the rest of the session. During the rest of the session, we used adults' natural responses (along with any behavioral accompaniments to the gesture such as vocalizations and facial expressions) to help judge whether chimpanzee gestures were imperative or declarative.

Declarative gesture was scored if chimpanzees produced a show, point, or give that served to direct the adult's *attention* in a sharing way to an object; *imperative gesture* was scored if they produced a give, point, or reach that served to request some *behavior* from the adult. Chimpanzees passed communicative gestures if they produced either a declarative gesture or an imperative gesture. Other imperative actions, such as taking E's hand and putting it on the toy, were also coded, but were used only in subsidiary analyses.

Obstacle Tests

Two obstacle tests were included to assess means-ends differentiation (physical) and very simple goal-detection (social).

Physical Obstacle

An attractive toy (e.g., a car or ball) was placed under a transparent box. Chimpanzees passed the physical obstacle test if they removed the box and obtained the toy.

34

Social Obstacle

One trial each of the *giving*, *blocking*, and *teasing* tests of Phillips, Baron-Cohen, and Rutter (1992) were used. Various small toys (e.g., tops, "slinkies," and balls) were used depending on the chimpanzee's interests. Gaze to E's face was coded during the approximately 5 seconds after E gave a toy to the chimpanzee, suddenly blocked the chimpanzee's play, or withdrew an offered object in a teasing fashion. Chimpanzees passed the blocking and teasing tests if they looked to E's face during those 5 seconds. They passed social obstacle if they passed either the blocking or the teasing test.

Object-Related Tests

Two object-related tests were included for comparison with the social-cognitive skills. They were expected to be unrelated to them developmentally.

Object Permanence

A series of object permanence tests was taken with some modifications from Uzgiris and Hunt (1975, tests 4, 12, and 14). All involved hiding a small toy under one or more opaque screens. E administered the easiest test (test 4) at the first session. If the chimpanzee responded correctly (i.e., removed the screen and obtained the toy) and then repeated the correct response in a second trial, E proceeded to the next test (test 12), and so on. Chimpanzees passed the object permanence test if they found the toy following one invisible displacement with two screens alternated (test 12). In this test, E placed a toy under one of two screens using a cup; the empty cup was then placed in the middle of the two screens.

Spatial Relations

Uzgiris and Hunt's (1975) spatial relations test 6 (utilizing the relation container-contained) was used. Chimpanzees were given a few minutes to play with a large cup and some wooden blocks. They passed spatial relations if they spontaneously placed two or more blocks into the cup and removed two or more blocks from the cup during their play.

Reliability

All sessions were coded live by the assistant who was present in the testing room during the session. Videotapes were used to resolve any questions. The live coder's scores were used for analyses in most cases because she had a better viewing angle. However, two of the skills, joint engagement and communicative gestures, were coded from videotapes because these could take place throughout the session and they often required several viewings in order to reach a decision. For all but these two skills, all (100%) of the tapes were recoded later from the videotapes by a single coder, who was blind to the hypotheses of the study, to assess interobserver reliability. For joint engagement and communicative gestures, one coder coded all the videotapes and another coded 25% of each chimpanzee's sessions for these two skills. Perfect (100%) agreement was achieved on the ages of emergence of the following skills: joint engagement, communicative gestures (and both imperative and declarative gestures separately), attention following (and point following separately), imitation of arbitrary actions, physical obstacle, and object permanence. The Cohen's κ's for imitative learning (0.79, with 91% agreement) and imitation of instrumental actions (0.77, with 94% agreement) were in the "excellent" range. The Cohen's κ for gaze following was in the "good" range: 0.73 (with 89% agreement). The only "fair" κ for spatial relations (0.43, with 83% agreement) resulted from a bad camera angle for the tape coder, but that was something that was easy to code live. For social obstacle, the coders agreed on the age of emergence for three of the four chimpanzees; for Mosi they disagreed. Again, the live coder had an advantage because she and E (with whom the chimpanzee was making eye contact) could discuss immediately whether the chimpanzee looked.

RESULTS

Results are presented in two parts. First, we describe how the chimpanzees performed on each of the individual measures. Second, we investigate the relative orders of emergence of the skills within and between individuals.

Individual Measures

We identified the age at the first testing session at which each chimpanzee passed each skill. These ages are presented in Figure 3. (Chimpanzees were not all tested at the same ages, and so it was not really possible to investigate mean ages of emergence of each skill.) The four main social-cognitive skills are listed in bold type in the figure, the components of each of those main skills are listed in regular type in parentheses underneath, and the other skills are listed in gray.

36

	Age of Emergence in Months																	
	5	6	7	8	15	17	19	21	23	25	26	27	30	36	40	44	48	not passed
Alex					SO PO	AF (gf, pf)	OP SR	CG (ig)										IL (ar,in) (ip) JE (dec)
Alexandra											*			SO PO IL (in) AF (gf,pf) OP	SR CG (ig)	(ip)		(ar) JE (dec)
Annet											SO PO IL (ar) OP			AF (gf,pf)	(in) SR CG (ig)	(ip)		JE (dec)
Mosi	SO			PO														all others

SO=social obstacle, PO=physical obstacle, AF=attention following (gf=gaze following, pf=point following), OP=object permanence, SR=spatial relations, CG=communicative gestures (ig=imperative give, ip=imperative reach/point, dec=declarative gesture), IL=imitative learning (ar=arbitrary, in=instrumental), JE=joint engagement

* testing was terminated after 10 minutes because she was uncooperative

FIGURE 3.—*Longitudinal study*: The age at the first testing session at which each chimpanzee passed each skill.

Joint Engagement

None of the four chimpanzees participated in a single episode of joint engagement in any session. Chimpanzees often looked to the experimenters but never did so spontaneously about a third object, just to share attention and interest to it.

Attention Following

Alexandra, Annet, and Alex all passed the overall attention following skill during one of their earliest testing sessions, and they all passed both the gaze and the point following tests. Interestingly, all three chimpanzees passed both of these tests for the first time in the same visit: Alex at 17 months and Alexandra and Annet at 36 months. Mosi did not pass any of these tests by the time of his final testing session at 8 months.

Imitative Learning

Only Annet and Alexandra passed the overall imitative learning skill. Annet passed both the instrumental and the arbitrary imitation tests, at 40 and 26 months, respectively. Alexandra only passed the instrumental test, at

36 months, and Alex did not pass either. Because it could be argued that requiring an expectant look to the end result following chimpanzees' response was too strict a criterion for the age of emergence of imitative learning, we also investigated when chimpanzees reproduced E's demonstration regardless of whether there was an expectant look. When this more generous criterion was used, Alexandra also passed the arbitrary imitation test, at 40 months, and Annet passed the instrumental imitation test one session earlier, at 36 months. Alex still did not pass imitation of arbitrary actions but did pass imitation of instrumental actions at 17 months. Mosi did not pass any of these tests, regardless of which criterion was used.

Communicative Gestures

Alexandra, Annet, and Alex all passed the overall communicative gestures skill. All three of them produced at least one type of imperative gesture, but none of them ever produced a declarative gesture. The first type of gesture produced for each of the three chimpanzees was an imperative give, at 40 months for Alexandra and Annet and at 21 months for Alex. Alexandra and Annet also produced distal imperative gestures, that is, reaching and/or pointing (Alexandra with middle finger extended and Annet with index finger slightly extended) imperatively at 44 months. These three chimpanzees also had many imperative gestures without looks to E, including some in which they manipulated E's body directly, for example, putting her hand on top of a box to ask her to open it (for Alex and Annet these were present already at their first testing sessions). Even when gestures without looks to E were included, Alex did not produce any distal imperative gestures, and still none of the chimpanzees produced any declarative gestures. Mosi did not produce any gestures of any kind, with or without looks to E, from 5 to 8 months of age.

Obstacle Tests

All four chimpanzees passed both the social and the physical obstacle tests very early. Alexandra, Annet, and Alex passed both tests during their first visit at 36, 26, and 17 months, respectively, and Mosi passed social obstacle at 5 months and physical obstacle at 8 months.

Object-Related Tasks

Alexandra, Annet, and Alex all passed both the object permanence and the spatial relations tests. Alexandra and Annet both passed object permanence during their first visit, before spatial relations. Alex passed both in the same session, at 19 months. Mosi did not pass either of these tests.

Summary

Overall, then, the most important finding on the individual level was that no chimpanzee ever spontaneously participated in an episode of joint attentional engagement and no chimpanzee ever produced a declarative gesture, either proximal such as showing or distal such as pointing. Otherwise—with the one exception of Alex for imitation when the most stringent scoring criterion was used—the three young chimpanzees were able to be generally successful on all of the social-cognitive skills tested.

Order of Emergence

Figure 4 presents for the three oldest chimpanzees the most common pattern of emergence for the four main social-cognitive skills as a group, along with the percentage of chimpanzees who displayed this pattern and the percentage of chimpanzees who passed each skill during the course of the study. The patterns for typically developing infants and children with autism from other studies are also included for comparison. In some cases, two or more skills emerged in the same month for individual participants, and so patterns of emergence across skills were based on skills that emerged *before or in the same month as* other skills. As was done with the children, the most common order shown by those participants whose skills emerged in different months was used to help disambiguate that of the other participants.

Mosi did not pass any of the main social-cognitive skills during his test sessions from 5 to 8 months of age. Two of the three other chimpanzees (67%), Alexandra and Annet, showed the same pattern: Imitative Learning → Attention Following → Communicative Gestures (and neither of them passed Joint Engagement). This percentage was significantly different from the percentage expected by chance (4%, binomial test, $p < .01$). If we do not require an expectant look to the end result for the imitative learning test, then Alex passed imitative learning at his second session as well, and then all three chimpanzees follow this pattern.

Chimpanzees' pattern resembled that of children with autism more closely than that of typically developing infants—in fact, with the exception of the skill of joint engagement, which no chimpanzee passed, it was identical to that of children with autism. On the level of individual subjects, chimpanzees' patterns segregated completely from those of typical infants:

Chimpanzees

Imitative Learning 67	→	Attention Following 100	→	Communicative Gestures 100	→	(Joint Engagement) 0

Individually, 67% of chimpanzees showed this pattern.

Typically-developing infants
(from Carpenter et al., 1998)

Joint Engagement 100	→	Communicative Gestures 100	→	Attention Following 96	→	Imitative Learning 96

Individually, 62.5% of infants showed this pattern.

Children with autism
(from Carpenter et al., 2002)

Imitative Learning 92	→	Joint Engagement 75	→	Attention Following 67	→	Communicative Gestures 58

Individually, 50.0% of children showed this pattern (this includes three children – 25% – who passed all five skills).

Numbers in the boxes are the percentages of participants who passed each skill during the course of the study.

FIGURE 4.—*Longitudinal study*: The most common pattern of emergence for the four main social-cognitive skills, and the percentage of participants who passed each skill during the course of the study. The patterns for typically developing infants and children with autism are also included for comparison.

no chimpanzee showed a pattern shown by any of the typical infants. For infants, joint engagement and communicative gestures (which for the vast majority of children were declarative gestures) led the developmental sequence whereas for chimpanzees communicative gestures (always imperatives) was at the end and joint engagement never occurred.

The object-related skills were included to test for things like general maturational effects as a possible explanation for any consistent ordering or relations found between the social-cognitive skills. Of the three chimpanzees who passed them, object permanence was passed by two chimpanzees between attention following and communicative gestures, and spatial relations was passed by all three of them between those same two social-cognitive skills, a more systematic pattern than was observed for human children. Interestingly, all three chimpanzees passed the physical obstacle task before (or at the same time as) the social-cognitive tasks (as did both groups of children). This fits with the hypothesis of Tomasello (1995) that subjects should display a differentiation between means and ends in their own behavior before understanding others' goals and intentions as measured by these social-cognitive tasks because one must experience a differentiation of means and ends in one's own behavior before understanding it through simulation in others' behavior.

Reliable patterns of emergence also appeared sometimes on the level of the individual tasks within the main skills. Table 2 presents these patterns, with those of typically developing infants and children with autism for comparison. For chimpanzees, within imitative learning, there was no consistent ordering between imitation of instrumental and arbitrary actions (whereas for both groups of children imitation of instrumental actions emerged first). Within attention following, gaze following and point following always emerged in the same month for chimpanzees, whereas point following preceded gaze following for both groups of children. Within communicative gestures, for chimpanzees imperatives always emerged before declaratives (since they never occurred)—which was also true of children with autism—whereas for typically developing infants declarative gestures emerged first. Interestingly, and unlike typically developing infants, for these chimpanzees comprehension of pointing preceded production of gestures, whereas infants produced gestures (mostly showing things to others) before comprehending the pointing gesture.

Finally, the social-cognitive skills were grouped according to their functions in terms of sharing, following, and directing attention or behavior. *Sharing attention* was operationalized as success on either joint engagement or declarative shows; *following attention* was operationalized as success on either point following or gaze following; *directing attention* was operationalized as success on declarative pointing; *following behavior* was operationalized as success on imitation of either arbitrary or instrumental acts; and *directing behavior* was operationalized as success on imperative gestures. Figure 5 presents the most common pattern of emergence of the skills at this level. Again, the patterns for typically developing infants and children with autism are also included for comparison.

When the two groups of children are compared, the main difference is that children with autism find it easier to follow and direct behavior than to follow and direct the attentional states of others. Chimpanzees go much further in this direction, as they never shared or directed attention at all. Within the behavior line, two of the three chimpanzees, Alexandra and Annet, showed the same order of following behavior (imitating) and then directing behavior with imperative gestures that typically developing infants and children with autism showed, which might suggest a similarity of process in understanding intentional action.

41

TABLE 2

ORDERING OF THE SOCIAL-COGNITIVE SKILLS' COMPONENTS FOR THE MAJORITY OF PARTICIPANTS IN EACH GROUP

	Chimpanzees	Typically Developing Infants	Children with Autism
Imitative Learning			
Attention Following	No consistent order	Instrumental → arbitrary	Instrumental → arbitrary
Communicative Gestures	Point following = gaze following	Point following → gaze following	Point following → gaze following
	Imperative → declarative	Declarative → imperative	Imperative → declarative

DISCUSSION

The three young chimpanzees in the study showed many similarities to human infants: they reproduced instrumental actions, they followed gaze, and gestured imperatively. But perhaps the most striking finding of this study was that not a single chimpanzee ever tried to share attention and interest with any of the human adults present. This was despite the fact that we included two situations at each session specifically designed to elicit declarative gestures and joint engagement, and we looked during the rest of all the sessions as well. In contrast, every typically developing infant in the Carpenter, Nagell, and Tomasello (1998) study shared attention and inter-

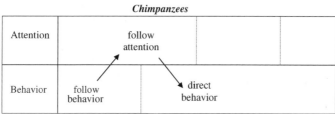

Individually, 67% of chimpanzees fit this pattern.

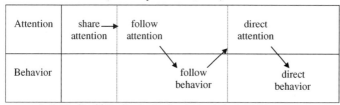

Individually, 83% of typically-developing infants fit this pattern.

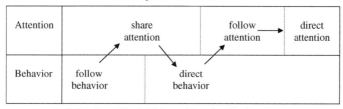

Individually, 67% of children with autism fit this pattern.

FIGURE 5.—*Longitudinal study*: Ordering of the social-cognitive skills by function. The patterns for typically developing infants and children with autism are also included for comparison.

est with an adult at their first session at 9 months by initiating joint engagement interactions in which they looked to the adult about an object and
sometimes actively showed objects to adults, and 83% of the infants had
produced a distal declarative gesture (point and/or communicative reach)
by the end of the study at 15 months. Indeed, even most (75%) of the
children with autism in the Carpenter et al. (2002) study participated in
joint engagement, although only 25% of them produced any declarative
gestures. This finding thus provides support for the idea that there is a
genuine human-ape difference in the motivation to share psychological
states, especially attention and interest, with others (see also Gomez, 1996).

Chimpanzees did not share, but each of them who was tested after 15
months did pass all or most of the other social-cognitive skills. Only Alex did
not pass imitative learning when the criterion of looking to the end result
expectantly was required; when it was not, he passed imitation of instrumental but not arbitrary actions. But perhaps if he had been tested during his
fourth year like Alexandra and Annet, he would have shown this skill as well.

Chimpanzees passed the different social-cognitive skills in a very reliable order. Depending on which criterion for imitation is used, either two of
three or all three of the chimpanzees developed the skills in the order:

imitative learning → *attention following* → *communicative gestures*
(with no joint engagement)

However, with no sharing, chimpanzees' developmental sequence of emergence of the skills was quite different from that of typically developing
infants in the Carpenter, Nagell, and Tomasello (1998) study. These infants
in fact showed the sharing skills—specifically, joint attentional engagement
and showing/declarative gestures—first, and even children with autism
quite often displayed at least some of these sharing skills as well (although
these children with autism were from the higher end of the spectrum). Like
children with autism, the chimpanzees found it easier in general to deal with
behavior than attention, but within the tasks concerned with behavior the
chimpanzees and both groups of children followed before they directed—perhaps suggesting a commonality of process with regard to the
understanding of behavioral actions only. Another difference between
chimpanzee and infant patterns was that the comprehension of communicative gestures emerged reliably before production of communicative gestures for chimpanzees (and the same was true for points in particular),
whereas the opposite order (or an inconsistent ordering in the case of
points) was found for infants.

With regard to individual differences, it is interesting to note that Alexandra and Annet, who were almost exactly the same age and had grown up
together, showed almost identical results in terms of the age at which they
passed most skills. One limitation of the study is that they were not tested

earlier, at the same ages as Alex, to enable a better comparison. But there were no ceiling effects, as very few skills were passed at chimpanzees' first visits. In general, concerning age, our data are not so rich, but four tests with Mosi from 5 to 8 months of age revealed none of the social-cognitive skills we were testing, and the first test with Alex at 15 months also showed none of the skills. And so Alex's following of E's point and gazes at 17 months of age, and his imperative giving at 21 months of age, are at the moment our best estimates as to when these skills begin to emerge in chimpanzees. These ages are one half year or more later than comparable ages of emergence in typically developing children. As with typically developing human children, the tested skills for each individual tended to emerge in a fairly short time window.

III. UNDERSTANDING INTENTIONAL ACTION

These longitudinal assessments enable us to identify the emergence of chimpanzees' earliest social-cognitive skills. But test batteries do not include all of the control conditions and task variations that are needed to characterize a cognitive skill more fully. We therefore also conducted a series of nine experiments, each with some kind of experimental and control condition. These experiments fall into three general content categories (corresponding to this and the next two chapters): chimpanzees' understanding of intentional action, their understanding of perception and attention, and their ability to participate in collaborative interactions involving joint intentions and attention.

In the initial set of full-blown experiments, we investigated three important steps in our three chimpanzees' understanding of intentional action. To test the understanding of others' goals, we investigated the comprehension of others' failed attempts and accidents. To test the ability (or motivation) to go down a level in the behavioral hierarchy to others' subgoals and means, we investigated the tendency to copy the particular "style" others use when acting. To test the understanding of others' intentions and rational choice, we investigated how subjects use information about constraints on the actor to decide whether to reproduce the means the actor used to achieve an end. In all cases, we used imitation/re-enactment methods to assess both the understanding of these different components of intentional action and also whether this understanding can be applied to learn from others.

FAILED ATTEMPTS

When an actor attempts to achieve a result but fails, there is a mismatch between the actor's goal and the environmental outcome. In this case, observers do not see the completed result but potentially can infer what the demonstrator was trying to do. The use of imitation as a response measure

46

allows us to determine what observers understand of the intentional action in these cases. If in the case of a failed attempt, observers reproduce exactly what the demonstrator did, then they apparently did not understand that he did not achieve his goal—they are just reproducing his surface behavior and not taking his underlying goals into account. If instead observers do what the demonstrator meant to do—perhaps in a different way—then they make it clear that they understood that the demonstrator had a goal that was not achieved.

This experimental approach was pioneered by Meltzoff (1995) with 18-month-old infants. Infants watched an adult either (a) successfully achieve a result with an object (e.g., pull apart two halves of a dumbbell) or (b) try but fail to achieve that result (e.g., while pulling, the adult's hands slipped off the ends of the dumbbell and it never opened). Infants produced the completed result equally often in both conditions, and they did so more often than in two control conditions in which they saw either no demonstration or the adult only manipulate the object. (Fifteen-month-olds have shown this same pattern of results; Johnson, Booth, & O'Hearn, 2001.) The inference here is that infants understood (i.e., they imagined) the adult's unachieved internal goal as she struggled unsuccessfully, and they then produced a result consistent with that, instead of copying the adult's surface behavior.

Bellagamba and Tomasello (1999) replicated these findings with 18-month-olds, but found that 12-month-olds did not reproduce the adult's intended result when they only saw a failed attempt. Bellagamba and Tomasello also added an additional End State condition in which infants saw the object already in its completed end state (e.g., the dumbbell already separated) and investigated whether, when then given the object in its initial state (e.g., dumbbell intact), they could perform the completed result without having seen any actions by the demonstrator. Both 12- and 18-month-olds found this difficult.

Two studies have used a similar procedure with chimpanzees. First, Myowa-Yamakoshi and Matsuzawa (2000; Experiment 1) showed five chimpanzees, all of whom had extensive experience with humans, a human experimenter first trying but failing to open a container, and then opening the container. Chimpanzees opened the container equally as often following failures as following successes, mirroring the Meltzoff (1995) finding with infants. However, results in the chimpanzee study are based on only two instances of opening in each condition. While this was numerically more than was found in an extended baseline control condition with different objects, it is not a very strong result.

Second, Call, Carpenter, and Tomasello (in press) used the same conditions as Bellagamba and Tomasello (1999) (with a no demonstration control instead of a manipulation control). In three experimental conditions, 50 chimpanzees (a) watched a chimpanzee demonstrator succeed in opening a tube, (b) watched a chimpanzee demonstrator attempt but fail to open the tube, or (c) discovered an already-opened tube in their enclosure without watching any demonstration. Again, chimpanzees opened the tube themselves equally as often, and equally as fast, in each of these conditions. However, chimpanzees also opened the tube at high rates in a control condition in which they saw no demonstration (or other information about the objects). This suggests the possibility that they solved the task using individual learning in all conditions.

It is thus unclear what chimpanzees understand about others' failed attempts, at least using imitation methods. There is some indication from a nonimitation method that they do understand something about trying but failing. Call, Hare, Carpenter, and Tomasello (2004) found that chimpanzees responded more impatiently when an experimenter was unwilling to give them food than when he was unable but trying to give them food. That is, chimpanzees gestured more to the experimenter and left the testing station earlier when, for example, he was eating a grape (unwilling) than when he was struggling to get the grape out of a container (unable), even though in both cases chimpanzees did not get the grape (see also Uller, 2004). In the current study, we knew from the longitudinal study that each of our three chimpanzees could imitate actions on objects. We thus used Bellagamba and Tomasello's (1999) procedure to investigate whether these chimpanzees would also show an understanding of failed attempts in an imitation context.

Method

Participants

Alex was tested at 35 months of age and Alexandra and Annet were both 53 months of age.

Materials

There were four sets of objects. Each set consisted of four different objects, each of which had a similar target action associated with it, so that we could test each of the four experimental conditions in each set and thus compare them across similar but different objects. One set of objects resembled the "cylinder and beads" objects from Meltzoff (1995): an object (a stick, a rope, a strap, or a chain) could be put through some sort of tube. Another set resembled the "prong and loop" objects from Meltzoff (1995): one object (a chain, two different loops, or a block of wood) could be hung on another object (various abstractly shaped apparatuses were used).

48

Another set resembled the "square and post" objects from Meltzoff (1995): an object (a wooden ring, a wooden square with a hole in it, a tube, and a wooden square with three triangular holes) was put on some sort of post. Finally, in another set, a hook or clip could be placed through a hole in some object.

After results indicated that with one of these sets of objects (the "cylinder and beads" set), chimpanzees' performance was too high in the Control condition, we replaced this set with a fifth set in which one object (a cup, a badminton birdie, a plastic rabbit, or a tennis ball with a hole in it) could be placed on another object (e.g., a stick or a triangle with a magnet attached). Figure 6 presents one example from each of the final four object sets, respectively, (a) in its initial state and (b) in its end state (i.e., what it looked like after the target action had been successfully completed).

Procedure

Table 1 presents the age at which each chimpanzee was first tested. The experimenter (E) sat on the floor facing the chimpanzee, who sat with a familiar caregiver. When the chimpanzee was seated quietly and paying attention, E brought out the first object and, while making sure that the chimpanzee was watching, E performed a demonstration on the object in one of four experimental conditions:

Demonstrate Target. E started with the objects in their initial state (objects apart). She demonstrated the target act (put the objects together) three times, then restored the objects to their initial state, and offered the objects to the chimpanzee. For example, E hung a wooden ring onto a metal post three times. E's successful actions were accompanied by soft excited vocalizations.

Demonstrate Intention. E started with the objects in their initial state (objects apart). She demonstrated the intention to perform the act, that is, tried but failed to perform the target act three times (chimpanzees never saw the completed end state), then offered the objects to the chimpanzee. For example, E aimed a wooden square toward a wooden post but missed three times, each time in a different direction. E's failed attempts were accompanied by soft disappointed vocalizations.

Demonstrate End State. E showed the objects to the chimpanzee already in their end state (objects together) for approximately the same amount of time as in the other demonstrations. She then quickly returned the objects to their initial state (objects apart) out of sight of chimpanzees, and then offered the objects to the chimpanzee. For example, E showed chimpanzees a tube already placed on top of a round wooden post, then covered the apparatus while she removed the tube. E's demonstration was accompanied by minimal interest vocalizations.

49

FIGURE 6.—*Failed Attempt Study*: One example from each of the final four object sets (a) in its initial state (before the demonstration) and (b) in its end state (i.e., what it looked like after the target action had been successfully completed).

Control Manipulation. E started with the objects in their initial state (objects apart). She then turned the objects around, looking at them from all sides, for approximately the same amount of time as in the other demonstrations, then offered the objects to the chimpanzee. E's demonstration was accompanied by minimal interest vocalizations.

Immediately following each demonstration, E gave the objects to chimpanzees and told them, "Now you," and they were given a response phase of approximately 1 minute, after which E moved on to the next object in the next experimental condition.

Chimpanzees participated in each of four experimental conditions with each set of objects, for a total of 16 trials (i.e., not counting the replaced trials from the "cylinder and beads" object set). Chimpanzees were originally tested on 4 consecutive days, with all four conditions on each day, using one object from each of the four object sets. The fifth, replacement set of objects was used 2 months later (again on 4 consecutive days, but with just one trial in a different condition each day). In any given condition, each chimpanzee saw the same, randomly chosen object, and chimpanzees received each of the conditions in the same order, which was counterbalanced across the 4 days.

Coding and Reliability

The main determination to be made was whether or not chimpanzees performed the target act, regardless of the condition they were in. This determination was made by a coder who was blind to condition, using the videotapes. Chimpanzees were coded as performing the target act, attempting to perform the target act (i.e., cases in which the chimpanzee was clearly trying to perform the target action but for mechanical reasons it did not work), or not performing the target act. Attempts and cases in which chimpanzees were credited with performing the target act were collapsed for analyses. In the Demonstrate Intention condition, we also looked for instances of mimicking E's demonstration (e.g., making the square miss the post).

A random selection of 50% of the sessions were also scored by an independent observer viewing the videotapes (eight trials each for each of the three chimpanzees, for a total of 24 trials). Perfect agreement was achieved.

Results

Figure 7 presents the number of times (out of four) each of the three chimpanzees produced the target action in each of the four experimental conditions. None of the chimpanzees produced the target action a single time in the Control condition. In the End State condition, there were just two productions, and so this condition did not segregate from the Control condition. In the Target condition, there was wide variability among chimpanzees, and so again this condition did not segregate from the Control condition. However, in the Intention condition all chimpanzees produced at least one target action, and so the distribution of performance in this

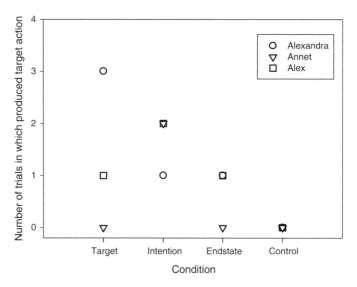

FIGURE 7.—*Failed Attempt Study*: The number of times (out of four) each chimpanzee produced the target action in each condition.

condition was higher than, and *did* segregate from, the distribution of performance in the Control condition. When the Intention condition is compared with the Control condition statistically, the result is: $t(2) = 5.00$, $p = .019$. Also of interest is the fact that the Target and Intention conditions did not segregate from one another. Further suggestive evidence that the chimpanzees understood that E was trying to do something other than what she actually did in the Intention condition is the fact that chimpanzees never, not once, performed the actual actions observed (mimicking failed attempts) in this experimental condition.

Discussion

The three juvenile chimpanzees in this study behaved very similar to 18-month-old human infants from Bellagamba and Tomasello (1999) in terms of the patterning of their responses across experimental conditions. For both species, the Target and Intention conditions were high and very similar, the End State condition was in between, and the Control condition was the lowest. The absolute values of imitation were higher for the infants, however. For example, the 18-month-olds in Bellagamba and Tomasello's (1999) study produced the target action about 80% of the time in both the Target and Intention conditions, whereas in the current study the young chimpanzees produced the target action in the same two conditions about half that often. But it is not clear how meaningful this comparison is, as the human infants also produced the target behavior 28% of the time in the Control condition, whereas the chimpanzees never produced the Target action in this condition— perhaps reflecting that the target actions were more "obvious" for the infants.

The current results represent the only reliable evidence to date that chimpanzees, or any other nonhuman animal, tend to reproduce not a demonstrator's actual surface behaviors but instead the demonstrator's intended act in a social learning situation. The Call et al. (2004) and Uller (2004) studies show some understanding of intended acts, but not in a social learning situation. The Myowa-Yamakoshi and Matsuzawa (2000) and Call et al. (in press) studies did take place in social learning situations, but they had the problem of a too high baseline in the Control condition (or not enough scorable experimental trials)—so that the results are basically uninterpretable.

Interestingly, there are many different cues that an individual might use to infer an actor's intended act. The current study has demonstrated only one—repeated attempts, as in Meltzoff (1995)—although in the current study this was accompanied by some minimal vocal indications of failure to meet the goal in terms of signs of frustration. Future research might profitably pursue the question of whether the range of cues that can be used to infer the goals behind actions are similar or different for humans and apes (see Carpenter and Call (in press), for a review of the cues human infants can use).

ACCIDENTS

Accidents, like failed attempts, are another case in which there is a mismatch between an actor's goal and the environmental outcome, and so they too are a good test of understanding of others' goals. In some sense, however, accidents are the exact opposite of failed attempts: in failed attempts an actor does not produce an outcome that he intends to produce and in accidents the actor produces some outcome without intending to do so. In practice, in imitation tests involving failed attempts, participants are shown the intentions but not the outcomes and must fill in the missing information, whereas in tests involving accidents, participants are shown the outcomes and must subtract out those that were not intended.

Carpenter, Akhtar, and Tomasello (1998) used this latter approach with human infants. They showed 14–18-month-old infants a demonstrator performing two actions on a series of objects, in counterbalanced order. In the key conditions, one of the demonstrator's actions was marked verbally as purposeful ("There!") and one was marked verbally as accidental

("Whoops!"), but otherwise the actions looked very similar. The two actions were then followed by an interesting result on the object, for example, the sudden illumination of colored lights. Instead of mimicking both actions they saw, infants reproduced the actions marked as purposeful significantly more often than those marked as accidental. Note that a strength of this procedure is that participants see the same actions in the different experimental conditions, so they can only use an understanding of goals or intentions (and not such things as their knowledge of object affordances, Huang, Heyes, & Charman, 2002) to solve this task.

Three studies have investigated chimpanzees' understanding of others' accidents, but none has done so using an imitation paradigm. These studies have produced mixed results. In the first, Povinelli and colleagues (Povinelli, Perilloux, Reaux, & Bierschwale, 1998; see also Povinelli, 1991) presented chimpanzees with two experimenters: one who tried to give chimpanzees juice but accidentally spilled it, and one who intentionally poured out the juice. They found that chimpanzees did not preferentially request the clumsy experimenter over the one who poured out the juice intentionally (except when this latter experimenter also threatened chimpanzees).

In a similar type of study, however, Call et al. (2004) found that chimpanzees responded differently when an experimenter offered them a grape but accidentally dropped it (he was unable to give the grape to them), as compared to when the experimenter offered the grape but withdrew it teasingly when chimpanzees reached for it (he was unwilling to give it to them), as did 9-month-old and older infants in the study of Behne et al. (2005). As in the case of failed attempts in this same experiment, chimpanzees gestured more and left the testing station earlier when the experimenter was unwilling to give them a grape than when the experimenter was unable to give it because of repeated accidents.

Finally, Call and Tomasello (1998) used an object choice paradigm to investigate understanding of accidents in chimpanzees, orangutans, and 2.5- and 3-year-old children. Participants were trained to use a marker (a wooden block) as a cue to which of three boxes contained a reward. Then, during the test phase, in each trial the marker was placed on two different boxes, one intentionally and one accidentally (in counterbalanced order). Each group of participants preferentially selected the intentionally marked box, again suggesting some understanding of intentional versus accidental action.

In the current study, we investigated whether chimpanzees would show an understanding of accidents in an imitation paradigm, using the general procedure of the Carpenter, Akhtar, and Tomasello (1998) study with human children. We used imitation as a response measure because it requires subjects to show precisely what they have understood the demonstrator to be doing intentionally (note that all three chimpanzees in this study were demonstrating around the same age that they could copy others' actions on objects in the longitudinal study).

Method

Participants

Chimpanzees were tested twice, approximately 1 year apart. Alex was tested at 16 and 28 months of age, and Alexandra and Annet were both tested at 36 and 47 months of age.

Materials

There were 14 tests at each of the two ages. For each of these 14 tests, a different apparatus was used. In each case, this consisted of a wooden box with two attachments to be manipulated and a reward. Instead of constructing 14 different boxes, we made four and covered them with different-colored paper or plastic for each test. Fourteen different pairs of objects were obtained from hardware stores and were attached to the left and right side of the top of each box. These attachments included latches, springs, knobs, wheels, spinners, bolts, doorknockers, flaps, and door stoppers; all of which were judged to be likely to be equally attractive to chimpanzees. One of four different types of rewards was attached to the back of each box: colored lights, a ball that fell out of a small box, a metal box that fell noisily, and a small sack of rice that fell into a box and made noise. See Figure 8 for a depiction of one of the boxes.

Procedure

The same general procedure as in Carpenter, Akhtar, and Tomasello's (1998) study was followed, except that there was no training phase. The chimpanzee sat with a familiar caretaker on the floor in a triangle with two experimenters, E1 and E2. When the chimpanzee was seated quietly and paying attention, E1 brought out the first box and placed it in front of the chimpanzee.

E1 then demonstrated two actions in succession on the box, for example, she moved a horizontal doorstopper up and down and then spun a wheel. One of the actions was always performed intentionally—it was followed by the German word "hier" ("here" in English)—and the other was always performed accidentally—it was followed by the German word "ups"

55

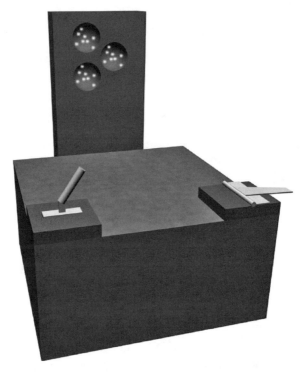

FIGURE 8.—*Accident Study*: One of the test boxes.

("whoops" in English) and a slight "jump" up of the body of the demonstrator. Otherwise, the actions looked the same whether they were performed intentionally or accidentally. For half of the boxes chimpanzees saw the actions presented in the order Intentional–Accidental (I–A), and for half of the boxes they saw the actions presented in the order Accidental–Intentional (A–I). These orders served as controls for each other: if chimpanzees reproduced only one of the two actions and they differentially reproduced the intentional action, regardless of its position in the sequence, it would indicate that they discriminated between the two types of actions and chose to copy the intentional one.

After E1 had demonstrated the two actions in succession once, E2 surreptitiously activated the reward (her hand was behind an occluder) for a few seconds. E1 then encouraged the chimpanzees to act on the box by saying "Now you." The response phase lasted until chimpanzees lost interest in the boxes or had played with them for approximately 1 minute. Then the same demonstration was repeated and another response period was given, after which E1 moved on to the next box.

During response periods, in both orders, the reward was activated by E2 when chimpanzees reproduced the intentional action, regardless of whether they reproduced the accidental action. In the A–I order, the reward was activated only if chimpanzees reproduced the intentional (second) action, regardless of whether or not they reproduced the accidental (first) one. In the I–A order, the reward was activated only if chimpanzees reproduced the intentional (first) action, regardless of whether or not they reproduced the accidental (second) action, but it was done so a full 2 seconds after chimpanzees' production of the intentional action in order to ensure that chimpanzees had time to produce the accidental action if they so desired.[4]

The boxes and objects were randomly assigned to the two orders, and occurred in alternating trials. All three chimpanzees saw the boxes in the same orders and the I–A and A–I orders were administered in the same way as well. Objects were paired with boxes in such a way that similar objects (e.g., a blue latch and a red latch) and actions (open/close latch) were used with intentional actions with half the boxes and accidental actions with the other half of the boxes. Each chimpanzee participated in a total of 28 trials, usually seven trials in each of the two orders at each of the two ages (because of experimenter error, Alexandra and Annet had one extra trial in the A–I order and one less trial in the I–A order). Chimpanzees were tested on 2 or 3 consecutive days at each age, with four to eight boxes on each day (with the same ordering and boxes at the two ages).

Coding and Reliability

Chimpanzees' responses were coded from videotapes. Only their first response in each trial was scored. A response consisted of one or more actions on the object(s) with no pause (defined as taking the hand(s) off the object and looking to the reward, or else receiving a reward). That is, if chimpanzees performed an action, then stopped and looked up to the reward before performing another action, then only the first action was scored. For each trial, chimpanzees were scored as reproducing the first action only, the second action only, both actions in order, both actions in the incorrect order, or neither action. These were then matched to the demonstrated orders for analyses. Attempts and partial actions (i.e., more than just touching the object) were included as reproductions.

Coding was carried out blind to experimental order. All (100%) of the trials were coded by an independent coder to assess interobserver reliability. Reliability was excellent: Cohen's κ was .92.

Results

Figure 9 illustrates how each of the three chimpanzees reacted to the two-act demonstrations comprising one intentional and one accidental act.

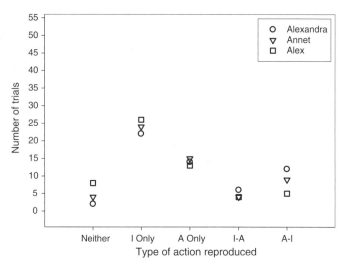

FIGURE 9.—*Accident Study*: The number of each type of intentional (I) or accidental (A) response.

There were a total of 56 different demonstrations for each chimpanzee, 14 in each of 2 years, each of which had two trials. It can be clearly seen from this figure that the chimpanzees imitated the intentional action more often than they produced any other response type, with the distribution of responses of this type clearly segregating from all the others. Statistically, the most straightforward analysis is to compare the two response types in which chimpanzees imitated only one of the two actions, and of course these again segregate. When the Intentional condition is compared with the Accidental condition statistically, the result is: $t(2) = 6.55$, $p = .012$.

In this study, chimpanzees had enough trials that the intentional and accidental responses of each individual could be compared quantitatively. Assuming an equal likelihood of producing an intentional only or an accidental only response, the one-tailed binomial probabilities of the response distributions depicted for each chimpanzee in Figure 9 are as follows (in all cases intention higher than accident):

Alexandra: $p = .243$
Annet: $p = .199$
Alex: $p = .053$

The likelihood of obtaining these three probabilities by chance, all in the same direction (Rosenthal, 1991), is highly unlikely (Zoverall = 2.53, combined $p = .011$).

58

In order to address concerns that perhaps our procedure of rewarding chimpanzees after they produced the intentional action led to chimpanzees learning to produce this action over time, we conducted two further analyses. First, we compared the first and second trials for each experimental box. Chimpanzees performed the intentional action only on 35 of their first trials and 37 of their second trials, not a large increase. Relatedly, for each set of 14 trials at each age separately, we split the trials in half and compared the first to the second half of trials. Chimpanzees performed the intentional action only on 38 of their first-half trials and 34 of their second-half trials (these numbers were 17 and 18 for the first age and 21 and 16 for the second age, respectively). Thus, if anything, they performed slightly worse over successive tasks. Second, across all trial administrations we compared performance in the I–A and A–I orders, that is, when the demonstrator showed the intentional action first versus second. The overall pattern of results was similar in the two cases, with intentional actions always being performed as often or more often than accidental actions.

Finally, to see if there was any change in responding across the two ages, we plotted responses separately for each age. The same general pattern of results was found at each age, except that at the younger age the distributions for the intentional action only and the accidental action only did overlap slightly (at the older age they did not).

Discussion

The three chimpanzees behaved very similarly to the 16-month-old human infants in the Carpenter, Akhtar, and Tomasello (1998) study. The infants produced the intentional action alone just under 60% of the time and the accidental action alone about 20% of the time; the chimpanzees produced the intentional action alone just under 50% of the time and the accidental action alone about 25% of the time.

Again, as in the failed attempts study just reported, the current results represent the strongest evidence to date that chimpanzees, or any other nonhuman animal, tend to reproduce a demonstrator's intentional but not accidental actions. Again, the Call et al. (2004) and Call and Tomasello (1998) studies represent evidence of chimpanzees distinguishing intentional and accidental actions outside of a social learning context, but the current study is the only one providing evidence for such a distinction as incorporated into a socially learned behavior.

The cues that the chimpanzees saw and presumably reacted to in the current study were somewhat different than those in the failed attempt study. Different verbal markers were present but chimpanzees probably used the startled bodily reaction (jumping up slightly) during accidental actions (which were also present in the Carpenter et al. study of human children).

COPYING STYLE

The chimpanzees in these two just-reported studies of social learning, as well as other apes in other studies outside of social learning contexts, thus appear to understand something about others' goals. They recognize when there is a mismatch between a human actor's goal and what actually happens, for example, in attempting to comprehend failed attempts and accidents.

The emphasis in those studies, however, was on the end result—whether the actor achieved the intended outcome or not. Another important aspect of an understanding of intentional action is the means by which the actor achieves the intended result. For example, an observer watches an actor using a stick to open a paint can. The observer understands the intentional structure of the action: the actor's goal is to open the paint can and the actor has chosen one behavioral means, among other possible means, for doing this. The observer can then either adopt the actor's means or not, as she chooses.

Human children often choose to adopt adults' means, even when these are not causally necessary. For example, Nagell, Olguin, and Tomasello (1993) showed that 2-year-old children copied an adult's flipping or no-flipping actions with a rake, even when that resulted in less efficient performance on their part. Similarly, Whiten, Custance, Gomez, Teixidor, and Bard (1996) found that 2–4-year-old children copied the particular actions an adult used to open a box, even though these actions were not causally effective.

Sometimes children go beyond choosing the same tool or arm movement as an adult and adopt even the particular "style" in which she used the tool or moved her arm (Hobson & Lee, 1999). Hobson and Lee (1999) proposed that children do this because they "identify" with others and so "assume (imitate) the expressive quality of" their behavior (p. 657). Typically developing children begin to do this around their first birthdays. Following the general idea of Hobson and Lee's study of older children, Tomasello, Petschauer, and Carpenter (in preparation) tested 6-, 9-, and 12-month-olds longitudinally on a series of imitation tasks. In each demonstration, the experimenter performed the action with a particular action style which was not necessary for achieving the demonstrated end result, for example, illuminated a light panel with the fist instead of the flat hand, or made a toy frog jump on the table with three distinctive jumps. Tomasello and colleagues coded whether infants reproduced the same end result, and whether they did so using the same unnecessary action style. They found that by 12 months infants were clearly copying the adult's action style more often than in a control condition.

Chimpanzees and other apes do not do this to the same extent as human children. They can be trained to mimic humans' actions, but they are unlikely to do this spontaneously, and they do not transfer this ability to other, instrumental tasks. For example, Hayes and Hayes (1952) trained their human-raised chimpanzee Viki to reproduce various body movements and gestures that they performed, for example, blinking the eyes or clapping the hands. They trained her using shaping and molding techniques, with rewards, throughout her daily life in their home for a period of more than 17 months before systematic testing began. After she had become skillful, some novel behaviors were systematically introduced. In general, she reproduced them faithfully and quickly; she had clearly "gotten the idea" of the mimicking game. More recently, Custance, Whiten, and Bard (1995) have demonstrated in a more rigorous fashion similar abilities in two nursery-reared chimpanzees after they were trained for a period of 3.5 months in a manner similar to Viki. Of the 48 novel actions demonstrated after the training period, one chimpanzee correctly reproduced 13 and the other correctly reproduced 20. Evidence that this is only mimicking comes from a study by Call and Tomasello (1995), who tested a human-raised orangutan who was trained in similar ways. This orangutan could copy novel body movements when told to "Do this," but he could not transfer these mimicking skills to a goal-directed action. When a demonstrator told him "Do this" and then showed him how to solve a problem involving an object (i.e., by manipulating a lever on a box in a certain way to obtain food), the orangutan did not copy the demonstrated action.

Instead of reproducing others' actions, chimpanzees usually reproduce the same end result as the demonstrator, without necessarily using the same means. There are many studies that show that chimpanzees (and other apes) focus on and learn something about—or else are more motivated to copy—the effects the demonstration produces on the environment as opposed to the actions the demonstrator used (see, e.g., Call & Carpenter, 2003; Tomasello, 1996, for reviews). One apparently contradictory study is that of Whiten et al. (1996), who presented chimpanzees with a transparent "foraging box" containing fruit. On any given trial, the box could be opened by one of two mechanisms, each of which could be operated in two ways. For each mechanism, a human experimenter demonstrated one way of opening the box to some subjects and the other way to other subjects, who were then given the chance to open the box themselves. Results were that for one mechanism there was no effect of the demonstration observed, and for the other mechanism there was some evidence that chimpanzees were more likely to use the manner of opening demonstrated by the experimenter. The authors claimed to have demonstrated that chimpanzees copied the action the experimenter used. However, in the analysis of Tomasello (1996), the chimpanzees could easily have learned how the different mechanisms worked via emulation learning, that is, by learning about the affordances of the mechanisms instead of the demonstrator's action.

There are some hints that apes who have been raised in human-like environments may be more likely to copy humans' actions than apes reared by their mothers. For example, Tomasello, Savage-Rumbaugh, and Kruger (1993) compared enculturated apes with nonenculturated apes on a variety of imitation tasks and found that enculturated apes reproduced both the demonstrator's means and ends more often than then nonenculturated apes. However, in this study, too, apes could have been learning about the affordances of the objects, and not the actions of the demonstrator.

We used the procedure developed by Hobson and Lee (1999) and modified by Tomasello et al. (in preparation) for younger children to test chimpanzees' tendency to copy a demonstrator's action style in an imitation task. The "affordances" explanation does not work so well in this study because in most cases the "style" aspect of the demonstrated actions involved specific hand movements or generic movements of the target object that do not constitute object affordances. We also tested deferred imitation by giving some demonstrations for which the subject's first opportunity to respond came 24 hours later.

Method

Participants

Chimpanzees were tested in three different sessions, with two visits each, during a period of 2–4 months (Alex between 16 and 17 months, and Alexandra and Annet at 35, 36, and 38 months).

Materials

A total of 36 objects, 12 at each of three sessions, were used. Objects varied widely and included toys and hardware items, for example: a toy telephone, a tape measure, various dolls, balls, and toy vehicles, a flour sifter, a trowel, and a tube (a detailed list can be obtained from the authors). Three conditions were tested in each session. Twelve sets of objects were compiled by randomly assigning objects with similar actions associated with them (e.g., rubbing, jumping, twisting) evenly across the different sets. This ensured that across conditions and sessions similar types of actions were performed. However, the sets of objects that were used in earlier sessions were easier to manipulate than the later sets. There were also many backup objects available. If chimpanzees performed the correct action during the Baseline period, that object was replaced with a new, backup object.

Procedure

Chimpanzees sat on the floor with a familiar caretaker facing the experimenter (E). At their first of two visits in each session, E began by giving the first object to chimpanzees. Chimpanzees were allowed to play with it for 30 seconds, as a Baseline period to see whether they would perform the to-be-demonstrated action spontaneously. If they did this, the object was replaced with another one and a new Baseline period was given with that object. If chimpanzees did not perform the assigned action, E then took back the object and performed the demonstration.

There were two experimental conditions and one control condition. In the Immediate condition, E demonstrated an action on the object twice and then gave the object to the chimpanzee for the response period. In the Delayed condition, E demonstrated an action on the object twice, and then put the object away without letting the chimpanzee touch it. The next day, E gave each of these objects to the chimpanzee in turn for a response period without any further demonstrations. In the Manipulation Control condition, E just looked at the object, turning it around and visually inspecting it from various angles, and then gave the object to the chimpanzee for the response period. Conditions were presented in the same randomly chosen order for all three subjects.

In the Immediate and Manipulation Control conditions, the response period lasted 15 seconds, after which E took the object back and put it away and went on to the next object. In the Delayed condition, after the demonstration, E immediately put the object away without letting chimpanzees touch it again. The next day, chimpanzees returned and were given each of the objects from the Delayed condition one by one for a 15-second response period with no further demonstration.

In the Immediate and Delayed conditions, E demonstrated the action with a particular, unnecessary action style that was not the most obvious way to perform the action or achieve the end result (but was still an easy action to perform). For example, she rubbed a doll in one direction with a flat hand, or pushed a light panel with her fist, or touched a tennis ball to her forehead three times, or rolled a roller with both hands.

Coding and Reliability

We were interested in two aspects of chimpanzees' responses: whether they achieved the same end result as E, and whether they did so using the same unnecessary action style E used. Each of these aspects was coded separately. For end result, we coded whether chimpanzees achieved the same end result as E (e.g., illuminated the light panel, regardless of how they did it), attempted to do so, or did not do so. For action style, we coded whether they used the same action E used (e.g., push with fist), attempted to do this, or not. Chimpanzees could get credit for using the same action style without getting credit for achieving (or attempting to achieve) the same end result (e.g., if they pushed the side of the lamp box or the floor with their fist). For the Manipulation Control condition, recall that each object had an assigned end result and action style that was similar to those in the other conditions for matching purposes across conditions. We coded to see whether chimpanzees produced these (undemonstrated) assigned end results and action styles in order to obtain the baseline probability of chimpanzees performing them after seeing any manipulation of the object.

Twenty percent of the tapes were coded by an independent coder, blind to the hypotheses of the study, to assess interobserver reliability. Excellent levels of reliability were achieved: Cohen's κ's for result and style at each session were both greater than .90.

Results

Figure 10 presents the number of times (out of 12) each of the three chimpanzees produced the target result in each of the three experimental conditions across the three testing sessions combined. Chimpanzees produced the target result in the Immediate condition an average of six times, whereas in the Manipulation Control condition they produced it an average of two times; the distributions clearly segregated. When the Immediate

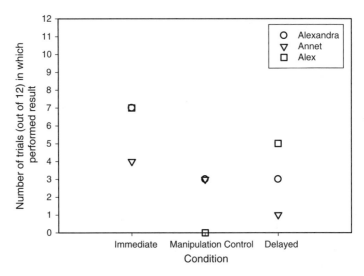

FIGURE 10.—*Copy Style Study*: The number of times (out of eight) each chimpanzee produced the target result in each condition.

condition is compared with the Control condition statistically, the result is: $t(2) = 2.31$, $p = .074$. The Delayed condition was not higher than the Manipulation Control condition, nor were the Immediate and Delayed conditions different.

Figure 11 presents the number of times (out of 12) each of the three chimpanzees copied the behavioral style of the demonstrator in each of the three experimental conditions. Each of the chimpanzees did this on only two of their 12 trials in the Immediate condition. The key comparison between the Immediate and Manipulation Control conditions showed no difference. Although two of the chimpanzees produced the style of the demonstrator slightly more when they saw it than when they did not, the distributions of these two key conditions did not segregate. The distribution of style responses in the Immediate condition did segregate from those in the Delayed condition, but the Delayed condition did not differ from the Manipulation Control condition in any type of comparison.

Discussion

In this study, the three chimpanzees produced the target result three times more often in the Immediate condition than in the Manipulation Control condition with a clear segregation of distributions. This finding is thus in general accord with previous findings that chimpanzees and other nonhuman primates are focused mainly on the results of a demonstrator's action, and are capable of reproducing that result themselves.

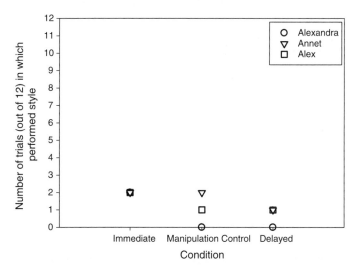

FIGURE 11.—*Copy Style Study*: The number of times (out eight) each chimpanzee produced the modeled style in each condition.

There was little evidence, however, that the chimpanzees copied the style with which the demonstrator performed the action. But style is a tricky concept. Thus, in the study of Tomasello et al. (1993) with enculturated and nonenculturated apes, there were always two possible actions on objects that the subjects might have reproduced—but this was not called style but rather the means or strategy (and note that the three chimpanzees in the current study also were reproducing others' means around the same age in the longitudinal study). The word style reflects the fact that it was not a necessary part of the instrumental action, not a part of the causal sequence, leading to the result. And so it is possible that the subjects of Tomasello et al. (1993) might have seen the actions of the demonstrator as instrumentally important (which experimenters intended them to be), and so copied them, whereas in the current study the subjects saw them as instrumentally unnecessary (which experimenters intended them to be), and so ignored them. The current results thus support previous research that behavioral means, strategies, and styles are mostly not salient aspects of intentional actions for chimpanzees, except perhaps those with much human contact in situations in which the behavioral means is considered to be instrumentally efficacious.

This pattern of results is in contrast to human infants, who in general seem much more attentive to the actual behavioral means, strategies, or style of the demonstrator. With particular reference to style, Tomasello et al. (in preparation) used exactly the same materials with human infants at 6, 9, and 12 months of age, and found that at 12 months of age infants copied the demonstrator's style more in the Immediate condition than in the Manipulation Control condition (19–6%). We do not know for certain whether the human infants (1) thought that the behavioral style was indeed instrumentally efficacious and so copied it for that reason (perhaps trusting the adult for this judgment) or (2) understood that the behavioral style was not an instrumentally efficacious part of the demonstration but copied it anyway in order "to be like adults." In either case, human infants seem to be more interested in, and so pay more attention to, the actual behavioral means, strategies, and style of others' instrumental actions.

RATIONAL PLANS

So human children often copy the means, and even the particular action styles, that adults use. But at least by their first birthdays, they do not always do this—they do not blindly mimic exactly what adults do. Instead, they take the adult's goal, and also situational factors, into account and copy the means only when it is important to the intentional action: when it is a

goal or sub-goal in and of itself. For example, Carpenter, Call, and Tomasello (2005) showed that 12- and 18-month-olds can copy an adult's hopping and sliding movements (and even sometimes the specific sound effects
she makes) when making a toy mouse move across a mat. However, when
infants see the exact same hopping and sliding movements (and hear the
exact same sound effects) when the mouse is moving across the mat in order
to end up in a toy house, infants do not copy those movements (or sound
effects), instead putting the mouse directly into the house. In that case,
infants apparently interpreted the adult's action in terms of this final goal
and so ignored the behavioral means—whereas in the first case they instead
saw the action itself as the adult's only goal and so copied it.

In the months immediately following their first birthdays, infants begin
to understand something more about others' means: that in pursuing a
goal, an actor may consider various action plans (means) and choose one to
enact in intentional action based on some "reason" related to reality. There
is only one study demonstrating such understanding in young infants.
Gergely, Bekkering, and Király (2002) showed 14-month-old infants an
adult touching her head to the top of a box to turn on a light. For half of the
infants, the adult's hands were occupied during this action (she was holding
a blanket around her shoulders) and for the other half the adult's hands
were free during the action. In both conditions, infants thus saw that the
adult was trying to turn on the light with her head. Nevertheless, when it
was their turn (and they had no blanket around their shoulders) infants who
saw the hands-free demonstration bent over and touched the box with their
heads more often than infants who saw the hands-occupied demonstration.
Apparently, infants assumed that if the adult's hands were free and she still
chose to use her head, then there must be a good reason for this
choice—she intended to turn on the light with her head—and so they
followed suit. However, if the adult's hands were occupied, then the use of
the head was explained away as necessary given her circumstance—without
the constraint of the blanket she would not have chosen this means—and so
they were free to ignore it as the same constraint was not present for them.
In this study, therefore, infants understood not just that the actor had a
means of action in mind, but also the reason why the actor chose the means
she did.

To test chimpanzees' understanding of the rational choice of means, we
sought a version of this task that was more instrumental and comprehensible to chimpanzees, and that did not involve copying a body movement.
We thus used something like Gergely and colleagues' similar "ball and
magnet" task (Király, 2002). In this task, an adult opened a box using an
unusual tool. In one condition (corresponding to the hands-free condition
above), the adult used the tool directly. In the other condition (corresponding to the hands-occupied condition above), before using the tool, the

adult first tried unsuccessfully to open the box with her hand. We would thus expect participants who understand the rational choice of means to use the tool in the first case but not the second, given that they themselves could use their hand in both cases. The understanding of the rational dimensions of intentional action involves more of an understanding of the "mental" processes involved. This has not been studied previously in nonhuman animals.

Method

Participants

Alex was tested beginning at age 41 months and Alexandra and Annet were both tested beginning at age 59 months.

Materials

There were two types of tools, string- and stick-like tools, which were designed to be very similar in size (25–35 cm long and thin) and function. There were four versions of each type of tool. String-like tools were: a piece of wooden wool (used for bedding in chimpanzees' cages), a piece of twine, a belt strap, and a strip of cloth. Stick-like tools were: a wooden cooking spoon, a block of wood, a strip of cardboard, and a strip of plastic. For demonstrations and response periods, a grape was tied to the end of the string or placed on top of the end of the stick. A large 40.5 × 40.5 cm transparent Plexiglas barrier was also used in one of the experimental conditions (see Figure 12).

FIGURE 12.—*Rational Plans Study*: The setup (Blocked condition).

There was a rectangular hole in the mesh at the level of chimpanzees' shoulders when sitting, to the frame of which a $77 \times 62 \times 60.5$ cm transparent Plexiglas box was attached such that it protruded outside of the enclosure. The chimpanzees' side of the Plexiglas box always had one of two transparent panels on it. During demonstrations, an intact panel was put there and during response periods, a panel with a 23.5×14 cm hole in the bottom was put there, through which chimpanzees could reach into the box. The main experimenter (E) sat to chimpanzees' right outside the enclosure (see Figure 12). The side of the box where E sat also could be opened and closed with a sliding transparent panel.

Procedure

Chimpanzees were in a familiar mesh enclosure; two experimenters, E and E2, were outside the enclosure. E and E2 were not familiar to chimpanzees so they spent time before testing feeding them and getting acquainted.

Chimpanzees were seen six times over the course of 5 weeks, for two warm-up sessions and eight experimental sessions. On the first visit, in order to make sure that they were willing to reach into the Plexiglas box, a series of grapes was placed by E2 in a location that was further away from where they would be placed during the tests, that is, 47 cm or more from the hole in the chimpanzees' panel. No tools or barriers were present at this visit. All three chimpanzees met the criterion of reaching for two grapes in this first session. At the beginning of each of the next sessions, chimpanzees were again allowed to reach for a grape at the location where the grape would be during the experimental trials (again no tools or barriers were present). Chimpanzees then also watched E reach into her side of the Plexiglas box and take three consecutive grapes (64 cm away from her—placed there previously by E2) with her hand, to show chimpanzees that she too could reach them from her position. E gave chimpanzees those grapes to eat.

Then the first test trial began. There were two experimental conditions. In the Blocked condition, E was prevented from reaching the grape with her hand by a barrier, so she used the tool to retrieve the grape. In the Not Blocked condition, there was no barrier and E could have reached the grape with her hand but she used the tool instead.

E2 put a grape onto the tool (and, in the Blocked condition, placed the barrier in front of E's opening), then left. E (who was at the other side of the room, distracted with other tasks during this) then approached and performed the demonstration, as follows:

Blocked. E repeatedly tried to reach through and around the transparent barrier for the grape. She then hesitated for a moment, taking another look at the situation, and then pulled the grape in slowly (with three short pulls) using the tool with the same hand she had tried to reach with before.

Not Blocked.   No barrier was present. E took a look at the situation, reached in, and pulled the grape in slowly (also with three short pulls) using the tool.

After each demonstration, E gave the grape to the chimpanzee and then moved to the corner of the room and did not pay attention to chimpanzees' responses. E2 returned, removed the barrier if applicable, and then rebaited the tool and reset the Plexiglas box so that E's side was closed and the chimpanzees could then reach freely into their side (they had no barrier in either condition). Then a sequence of three response periods was given, after each of which E2 rebaited the tool. A second demonstration in the same condition with the same tool, and then three more response periods, followed. Chimpanzees always retrieved the grape immediately.

Chimpanzees received two sets of two models and six response periods with each type of tool (string and stick) in each of the two experimental conditions, for a total of 24 trials in each of the experimental conditions. Tool sets and experimental conditions were perfectly counterbalanced within subjects. Order of conditions was randomized within sessions and the same for all three subjects.

Coding and Reliability

For each response period, we coded whether chimpanzees used the tool to pull in the grape. We also coded whether they first touched the grape or the tool, or touched the tool at all. Coding was carried out using videotapes. To assess interobserver reliability, an independent coder coded 33% of the videotapes, blind to condition. Perfect agreement was achieved: Cohen's κ's for each measure were 1.0.

Results

Figure 13 presents the number of trials (out of 24) in which each of the three chimpanzees used the tool to bring the grape into reach in each condition. Alexandra used the tool approximately equally often in the Blocked and the Not Blocked conditions. Annet used the tool more than twice as often in the Not Blocked as in the Blocked condition, and Alex did this slightly more often. Comparing the three chimpanzees in the two experimental conditions, we find that the conditions do not segregate. Also,

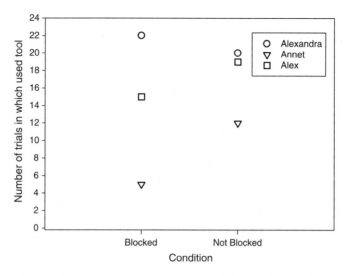

FIGURE 13.—*Rational Plans Study*: The number of trials (out of 24) in which each chimpanzee used the tool to bring the food into reach.

Annet's results are not significantly different from chance by themselves (McNemar Test, $p > .10$, including also in the analysis, as complement, the number of trials in which she used her hand to get the grape). The same comparisons were also performed with the two other dependent measures: the number of trials in which the chimpanzees touched the tool at all during the trial (a more generous measure) and whether the chimpanzees first touched the tool or the food. The same pattern of results was found again in these cases (including for Annet as an individual).

Discussion

Human infants of only 14 months of age, in an analogous task, used a tool more often in the Not Blocked than in the Blocked condition (Király, 2002; see also Gergely et al., 2002 for a similar task). The proffered explanation is that the infants interpreted the use of the tool as forced by the adult's situation in the Blocked condition, and as that situation did not apply to them (their reach was not blocked) there was no reason for them to use the more effortful means. However, if the adult used the tool when, by all appearances, she might just as easily have used her hand directly, then infants tended to copy her more effortful means—apparently thinking that she must have had a good reason, even if they could not see what it was. In the current study, one of the chimpanzee subjects clearly did not follow this same pattern, and while the other two tended to, this difference was so small

71

that chance cannot be ruled out as an explanation. This is clearly not sufficient evidence to draw positive conclusions about chimpanzees' skills in this task.

There is thus still no clear evidence that chimpanzees understand that people act rationally, choosing means to achieve their goals that are appropriate for the reality situation at hand. On the other hand, one also cannot draw definitive negative conclusions on the basis of a single task. We also tried another, analogous task, but the chimpanzees tended to simply reach directly for the food in all cases—and so the task was inappropriate for investigating the effect of the independent variable. Therefore, although it is advisable that we wait for further tests before drawing definitive conclusions, at the moment, although chimpanzees can understand some aspects of human intentional action (e.g., failed attempts and accidents), we have no evidence that chimpanzees analyze human intentional action down into the reasons why actors chose the means that they did in a particular situation.

SUMMARY AND DISCUSSION

Across the four studies in this section, a fairly coherent picture emerges. Chimpanzees are good at reproducing the desired end result of another's action, and indeed they can even produce this desired result (corresponding to the internal goal) even when it was never observed. They also can ignore unintended results, produced by accident, again showing sensitivity to the internal goal. However, the chimpanzees in these studies did not attend to the behavioral style used by the human demonstrator, and showed no strong tendency to analyze the demonstrator's intentional actions in terms of the rational reasons the demonstrator had for choosing one means over another. Chimpanzees' analysis of goal-directed action, then, may operate mainly on the level of the internal goal the actor is striving to achieve; chimpanzees may not delve deeper into the rational dimensions of the process to explain why actors chose the means that they did in pursuing their goal.

NOTE

4. In several cases, E2 erred and activated the reward too early, but the same pattern of results is found when these trials are dropped from analyses.

IV. UNDERSTANDING PERCEPTION AND ATTENTION

There have been many studies that show that chimpanzees can follow others' gaze (e.g., Itakura, 1996; Povinelli & Eddy, 1996; Tomasello, Call, & Hare, 1998). There are at least two possible explanations of this behavior. First, it could be that chimpanzees respond automatically to others' head turns by turning their own head in the same direction. Or second, it could be that chimpanzees understand that others see things and that if they look in that direction they will see what the others see. There are several further studies of chimpanzees that suggest that the latter explanation is the correct one. We test the current group of chimpanzees with some of those studies. First, we tested whether they would follow a human's gaze to an out-of-sight location behind a barrier. Second, we tested what they understood about the mechanism by which people see, that is, whether they knew that people could see them only when their eyes were open and facing them.

Another question that has not been addressed so far with chimpanzees is whether when they see someone looking at an object they understand that the other can be attending to any of multiple possible aspects of the object. This understanding of *attention* goes beyond understanding of seeing and perception, and involves knowing what someone is looking at even when gaze direction is not diagnostic. We also tested this understanding in our three chimpanzees.

FOLLOWING GAZE AROUND BARRIERS

Simple gaze following is not sufficient evidence that the observer knows that the looker sees something. It might be that co-orientation is a built-in response for the species, or it might be that individuals learn individually that when they look in the same direction as another individual they often find something interesting there. In studies with human infants, therefore, other indicators and experimental setups are used. For example, if infants look in the direction of another and see nothing interesting, they "check back" with the adult, looking at her face again and back to the location

(Butterworth & Cochran, 1980). By 18 months, when following gaze infants do not stop at the first thing they see, but instead follow gaze past distractors (Butterworth & Jarrett, 1991). But most telling, infants from 12 months of age follow the direction of another's gaze to out-of-sight locations behind barriers, actually locomoting some distance to put themselves in a position from which they can see what the adult is seeing (Moll & Tomasello, 2003). This paradigm is especially diagnostic, it would seem, because it not only involves a kind of representation of what the other might see, but also something in the direction of perspective-taking.

Chimpanzees follow gaze, and even sometimes "check back" to see if they followed correctly (Call, Hare, & Tomasello, 1998)—but this checking back normally only occurs after 3 or 4 years of age (Bräuer, Call, & Tomasello, in press). Adult chimpanzees also follow gaze past distractors and even around barriers (Tomasello, Hare, & Agnetta, 1999). These studies suggest that at least by the time they are adults, chimpanzees, like human infants, understand that others see things, and even that they are motivated to see what others see. But there are no systematic data involving such things as barriers and distractors with younger chimpanzees. In the current study, therefore, we used the barrier procedure of Bräuer et al. (in press; very similar to that of Moll & Tomasello, 2004, with human infants) as a test of whether our young chimpanzees understood seeing. Each of these chimpanzees had already passed tests of following others' gaze 19–20 months before in the longitudinal study.

Method

Participants

Alex was tested at age 37 months and Alexandra and Annet were tested at age 55 months.

Materials

Four natural barriers in chimpanzees' sleeping cages were used. Figure 14 presents a depiction of each one, and the space available to the chimpanzee subject (the chimpanzee is depicted in the starting position and arrows show where it had to go to see what E was looking at). Pieces of fruit were given to chimpanzees between trials to encourage them to return to the same starting position in front of the experimenter for each trial.

Procedure

The experimenter, E, sat outside the chimpanzee's enclosure, separated by mesh. She fed the chimpanzee a series of pieces of fruit. Then, she

(a) Window

(c) Under

(b) Door

(d) Under left

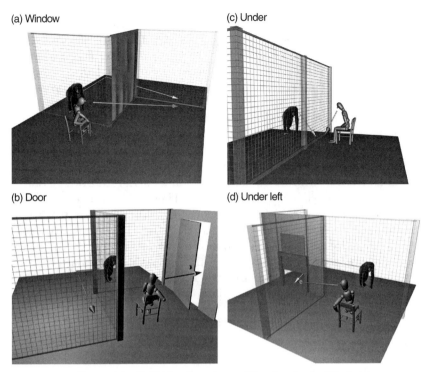

FIGURE 14.—Following Gaze Around Barriers Study: The barriers.

suddenly looked to one of five predetermined locations for 1 minute, alternating gaze between the location and the chimpanzee many times, and making an excited grunting noise. She called the chimpanzee's name occasionally, if needed, to get the chimpanzee to pay attention.

In the control test, the location E looked at was the ceiling. In the experimental tests, she looked at one of the following four locations:

Window: The window to chimpanzees' left was covered with cloth so that chimpanzees could not see through it. E leaned over and looked behind the covered window. Chimpanzees had to move behind and to the left to be able to see what E was looking at.

Door: The door into the testing room was only half open so chimpanzees did not have a direct line of view to the corridor outside. E leaned back to look through the door into the corridor. Chimpanzees had to move to the left approximately 2–3 m to a different cage to be able to see what E was looking at.

Under: There was a frame on the cage between the wire mesh and the floor. Under that frame was a small gap of about 2 cm. E bent down and looked down under the frame on her side of the mesh. Chimpanzees had to bend down and look through the gap to see what E was looking at.

Under-Left: There was another frame to the right of chimpanzees, below the guillotine door leading to the other cage. Under that frame was a small gap of about 2 cm. E looked diagonally under the frame. Chimpanzees had to approach the frame to see what E was looking at.

After E had looked to the location for 1 minute, she stopped and she and the chimpanzee took a break, which included giving chimpanzees a piece of fruit, regardless of what they had done during the trial.

For each of the four types of barriers, chimpanzees received three experimental trials in which E looked behind the barrier and three control trials in which E looked instead at the ceiling. These trials were conducted in six sessions of four trials each (two experimental and two control trials, alternating, in counterbalanced order across sessions), for a total of 12 trials in each condition. In order to minimize habituation, test sessions were spread out over a period of 3 weeks, with 2 consecutive test days, 1 week break, 2 test days, 1 week break, and 2 final test days. All three chimpanzees experienced the conditions and locations in the same order.

Coding and Reliability

All trials were scored from the videotapes. We were interested in whether chimpanzees looked to see what E was looking at. In many trials, we could see this clearly—chimpanzees moved to the location from which it was possible to see what E was looking at, and they clearly looked in that direction themselves. But in other trials, because of the arrangement of the mesh, frames, windows, and the camera angle, it was difficult to tell with certainty precisely where chimpanzees were looking. We thus had coders note all looks to the correct location, and in addition indicate for each look whether they were "sure" that the look was to what E was looking at or whether they were "not sure." We also coded latency to the first "sure" look, and latency to the first of either type of look. Finally, because we noted that chimpanzees also sometimes showed clear evidence of searching behavior, we also coded any instances of looking to what E was looking at and then looking back up at E's face in a checking way.

A second coder, blind to the hypotheses of the study, coded 25% of the tapes to assess interobserver reliability. For looks (of either type), excellent agreement was achieved: Cohen's $\kappa = .78$. For the coders' judgment of "sure" or "not sure" the Cohen's κ was in the good range (.66), as was the κ for search behavior (.68). For latency, the correlation between the two coders' scores was .99 ($n = 7$, $p < .001$) and there was no significant difference between them, $t(6) = .33$, $p = .75$.

76

Results

Figure 15 displays the proportion of trials in which the coder was "sure" that each chimpanzee clearly looked behind the barrier where E had looked. They did this on an average of 44% of the 12 experimental trials as compared with only 3% of the 12 control trials, the distributions thus segregating totally. When the Experimental condition is compared with the Control condition statistically, the result is: $t(2) = 5.00$, $p = .019$.

In this study, chimpanzees had enough trials that the number of times subjects looked where E looked in the two conditions could be compared quantitatively for each individual using Fisher's exact probability tests (two-tailed). Assuming an equal likelihood of looking in the experimental and control conditions, the experimental value is higher than the control value for each individual with the following probabilities:

Alexandra: $p = .005$
Annet: $p = .14$
Alex: $p = .09$

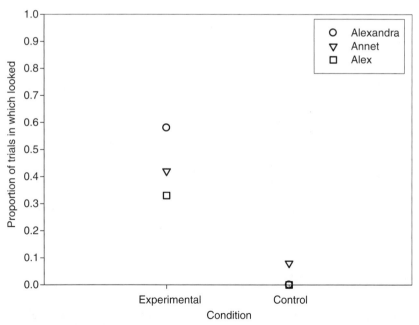

FIGURE 15.—Following Gaze Around Barriers Study: The proportion of trials in which each chimpanzee looked behind the barrier where E had looked.

The likelihood of obtaining these three probabilities by chance, all in the same direction (Rosenthal, 1991), is highly unlikely ($p < .001$).[5]

As an additional measure, we also looked at the latency from the time the cue was given until the time the chimpanzee looked (for those trials in which they looked). Chimpanzees took an average of 35 seconds to look in the Control condition (this was the value just for Annet, who was the only one to look in the Control condition), whereas they took an average of 26.7 seconds to look in the Experimental condition (with all three chimpanzees' means being lower than the one control value: Alexandra = 27.1, Annet = 20.2, Alex = 32.8).

Finally, all three chimpanzees engaged in search behavior in the Experimental condition (Annet and Alex did this in 33% of trials and Alexandra did it in 17% of trials), but none of them ever engaged in search behavior in the Control condition.

Discussion

The three chimpanzees in this study clearly followed the humans' gaze behind barriers. This is not so surprising as other studies have found that even chimpanzees with little human contact nevertheless still follow human gaze behind barriers (Tomasello et al., 1999; Bräuer et al., in press). But the current results demonstrate that this ability is present by 3–4 years—much younger than in those experiments—at least for apes who have grown up in the midst of human social interaction.

In the one study of this phenomenon with human infants, Moll and Tomasello (2003) found that infants at 12 months of age followed gaze behind barriers approximately 25% of the time, whereas infants at 18 months of age followed gaze behind barriers approximately 75% of the time. Our three chimpanzees did this about 63% of the time, in between these two values. The interpretation of this phenomenon is not totally straightforward even in the human infant literature, but on one interpretation it provides evidence that the subject wants to see what the looker sees, that is, that the subject understands that the looker can see something that it cannot. In a rich interpretation, this behavior might even suggest something like Level 1 perspective taking (Flavell, 1977), as the subject has to move to a new place to match the looker's viewing angle.

MECHANISMS OF PERCEPTION

Human infants and chimpanzees (and our three young chimpanzees in particular) can follow others' head turns, and even look past barriers and distractors to identify what the other is looking at. But there is more to an understanding of others' perception. Infants as young as 12 months of age also show that they understand something about the mechanism by which people see. Brooks and Meltzoff (2002) found that 12-month-olds followed gaze more when an adult turned her head with her eyes open than with them closed. Fourteen-month-olds looked more when the adult's eyes were unobstructed than when they were covered by a blindfold. Fourteen- and 18-month-olds also follow eye gaze direction and not just head direction (Caron, Butler, & Brooks, 2002; Corkum & Moore, 1995; Moore & Corkum, 1998).

Chimpanzees have been tested several times on their understanding of eyes as the mechanism by which others see, with mixed results. For example, Povinelli and Eddy (1996; see also Reaux et al., 1999) presented chimpanzees with two experimenters who were oriented to the chimpanzees in different ways, for example, one facing the chimpanzee and one with the back turned, and they coded from which experimenter chimpanzees requested food. Chimpanzees distinguished between the experimenters based on body orientation, not head or eye orientation, begging more from the experimenter whose body was facing them. However, when tested in a similar situation but with the important methodological change that there was one experimenter with different orientation states across trials instead of two experimenters with different orientation states simultaneously, chimpanzees behaved differently. Kaminski et al. (2004) found again that chimpanzees (aged 8–26 years) distinguished based on body orientation, but also found some sensitivity to face orientation: when the experimenter's body was facing them, chimpanzees begged more when that experimenter's face was turned toward them than when it was turned away. This sensitivity was limited to cases in which the experimenter's body was oriented towards them—they did not show this difference when the experimenter's body was facing away from them. They also did not distinguish between eyes open and eyes closed in this situation.

There is some evidence that apes raised by humans may have a more complex understanding of the role of the eyes in others' perception. Call and Tomasello (1994) and Gómez (1996) found that one orangutan and three chimpanzees raised with substantial human contact did differentiate and behave appropriately to humans with their eyes open and closed. We used the procedure of Kaminski et al. (2004) to test our chimpanzees, who were again younger than those in previous studies. In a first experiment, we tested whether chimpanzees begged more for food when an experimenter was looking at them directly than when the experimenter was turned away (either head or whole body facing away) or absent. In a second experiment, we tested the effects of eye and face direction more specifically.

EXPERIMENT 1

Method

Participants

Alex was tested at age 37 months and Alexandra and Annet were both tested at age 47 months.

Procedure

The experimenter (E) was not familiar to chimpanzees. After engaging in a warm-up period with the chimpanzee, he sat facing the chimpanzee through the enclosure. Two bowls of fruit were placed on the floor outside of chimpanzees' enclosure near E. Chimpanzees could see the bowls but not reach them.

There were two types of trials: filler trials and experimental trials. In filler trials, E gave the chimpanzee a piece of fruit through the mesh normally; in experimental trials, E looked at a specified location for 40 seconds without giving chimpanzees any fruit (see below for conditions). The session began with a filler trial. When the chimpanzee was sitting on the floor across from E and relatively calm and focused, E began the first assigned experimental condition. There were four experimental conditions:

Eyes Open: E looked at the chimpanzee with his eyes open.

Head Turned: E's body faced the chimpanzee but his head and eyes were turned away to the left side, looking at the back wall.

Back Turned: E sat with his back turned to the chimpanzee.

Absent: E left the room, closing the door, and waited outside.

E held his position (eyes open, head or back turned, or outside the room) for 40 seconds without responding to any behaviors by the chimpanzees (but calling their name and talking to them, noncontingently, throughout). At the end of the 40 seconds, he gave chimpanzees pieces of fruit from the bowls if they were requesting it at that moment; if not, he waited until they requested it. He then went on to the next filler trial, and then the next experimental trial.

Chimpanzees were tested in each of the four experimental conditions on each of four different days, in counterbalanced order across days. All three chimpanzees participated in the conditions in the same order. There were thus a total of 16 experimental trials, four in each of the four conditions.

Coding and Reliability

Chimpanzees' behaviors during the 40-second experimental trials were coded from videotapes. A list of all relevant behaviors was generated (taken from Kaminski et al., 2004). These included: sticking fingers or hand through the mesh, banging against the Plexiglas, clapping hands, presenting body for grooming, swinging against cage at E, and displaying. Only behaviors that were directed at E were counted (i.e., behaviors that took place when chimpanzees were near and visible through the Plexiglas panel that separated them from E, and that included eye contact with E). The frequencies of each of the behaviors were summed together for analyses.

An independent coder coded 20% of the videotapes to assess interobserver reliability (for both Experiment 1 and Experiment 2 together). An excellent level of reliability was achieved: Cohen's $\kappa = .84$.

Results

Figure 16 presents the number of times each of the three chimpanzees gestured or directed behavior at E in each of the four conditions in this experiment. Looking at individuals, each chimpanzee gestured more often when E was looking at them (Eyes Open control) than in each of the conditions in which E was looking away; that is, for each individual the Eyes Open control condition segregated from the three other conditions. When each experimental condition is compared to the Eyes Open control con-

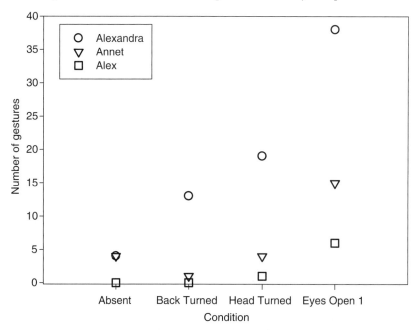

FIGURE 16.—Mechanisms of Perception Study: Number of gestures in each condition in Experiment 1.

dition, the following statistics result: Out of Room: $t(2) = 1.97$, $p = .094$; Back Turned: $t(2) = 2.72$, $p = .057$; Head Turned: $t(2) = 2.88$, $p = .052$.

EXPERIMENT 2

Chimpanzees thus knew when E was looking at them, and they gestured more to him in this case. In the next experiment, we tested whether they knew the importance of the eyes being open and the face turned toward them. One tricky issue in this next experiment is the condition we call "Over shoulder," when E can potentially see chimpanzees' gestures, but he is not really in a position to hand over the food easily. In this condition, we might expect intermediate amounts of gesturing, as found by Kaminski et al. (2004).

Method

The same materials, design, and general procedure were used as in Experiment 1. The only difference was the conditions. In the current experiment, E behaved as follows in each experimental condition:

Eyes Open: E looked at the chimpanzee with his eyes open (as in Experiment 1).

Eyes Closed: E faced the chimpanzee in exactly the same way as in the Eyes Open condition, but with his eyes closed.

Head Up: E sat facing the chimpanzee with his eyes and head oriented up to the ceiling.

Over Shoulder: E sat with his back to the chimpanzee, but looked at the chimpanzee by turning his head over his right shoulder.

Results

Figure 17 presents the number of times each of the three chimpanzees gestured or directed behavior at E in each of the four conditions of the second experiment. Looking at individuals, Alexandra and Alex gestured more when E was looking straight ahead (Eyes Open control) than they did in the other conditions; but Annet did not. When each experimental condition is compared with the Eyes Open control condition, the following statistics result: Over Shoulder: $t(2) = 1.85$, $p = .103$; Head Up: $t(2) = 1.50$, $p = .137$; Eyes Closed: $t(2) = 1.40$, $p = .149$.

Discussion

Povinelli and Eddy (1996) concluded that chimpanzees do not understand whether a potential recipient of their gesture can or cannot see them.

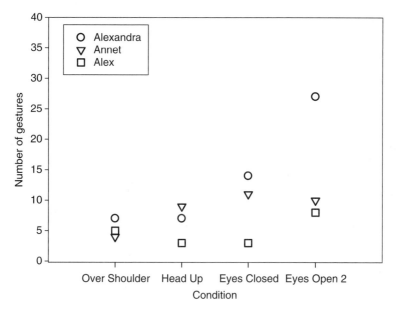

FIGURE 17.—Mechanisms of Perception Study: Number of gestures in each condition in Experiment 2.

The problem, as indicated above, is that chimpanzees were required in their study to choose between communicative partners—a highly unnatural situation. In the study of Kaminski et al. (2004), on which the current study was based, subjects did not have to make a choice on a given trial, but rather the comparison was between conditions across trials. Using this procedure, the current study provides moderately strong evidence that chimpanzees do indeed know when their communicative partners can and cannot see them and are ready to give them food—although not in the Eyes Closed condition. Again, the current study demonstrates this ability at a younger age than previous studies (in which the youngest apes were 8 years old), at least for chimpanzees with much human experience.

We know of no study of this type with human children, other than that of Povinelli and Eddy (1996), who used the same unnatural method they used with chimpanzees in which the subject has to choose who to communicate with. Children balked at this procedure, and indeed had to be trained in an arbitrary response (placing their hand on the table, matching a drawing of a hand, in the direction of one adult or the other) in order to finish the study. We thus do not know in this case how our three subjects' performance compares to that of human children at any age. But it is perhaps noteworthy that when they are pointing for adults, infants of 15 months of age look to the adult for reaction only after they point, whereas infants of 18 months of age often look to the adult before pointing, perhaps to make sure she is attending first (Franco & Butterworth, 1996).

UNDERSTANDING ATTENTION

It thus seems that chimpanzees know something about what others see. But when people look toward a group of several objects clustered close together, they may see them all but, for reasons related to their current goal, only attend to one of them. To go even further, one could look at a *single* object and focus on one or another aspect, including the object as a whole, some part of it, its color, its shape, its texture, and so on.

Two recent studies have investigated young children's understanding of this type of selective attention. First, Tomasello and Haberl (2003) had a female adult say to 12- and 18-month-old infants "Oh, wow! That's so cool! Can you give it to me?" while gesturing ambiguously in the direction of three objects. Two of these objects were "old" for the adult—she and the child had already played together with them—and one object was "new" to her (though not new to the child). Infants gave the adult the object that was new for her. This suggests that they understood that even though the adult was oriented to all three objects equally, she was selectively attending only to the one that she had not previously experienced and so now wanted. One interpretation of this result is that infants understand perception as a kind of rational action, in the sense that from all the things that they see, people can choose to attend to only a subset, and they do this for reasons related to their goals.

Second, in a current study in our laboratory, Moll, Koring, Carpenter, and Tomasello (submitted) used a similar but different procedure and found that 14- to 24-month-old children reacted in a similar way even when only a single object was involved. In this case, a female adult approached a single object and exclaimed "Oh, wow! Look at that!" while looking at it. In half the trials the adult and child had already played together with the object—the object was old for the adult—and in half the trials it was new to the adult (but not the child). When the object was old to the adult, children treated her exclamation as referring to a specific aspect of the object: they walked around and inspected the adult's side of the object, or else looked around the room for some other possible referent, apparently inferring that the adult could not be referring in such an excited way about something she had played with just a moment ago. In contrast, when the object was new to the adult, children took her response as directed at the object as a whole and did not search for other possible referents.

This type of attention understanding has not yet been studied in non-human animals. In the current study, we used the Moll et al. (submitted) procedure to test whether, along with understanding something about oth-

84

ers' visual perception, chimpanzees also understood something about others' selective attention.

Method

Participants

Alex was tested at 37 and 41 months of age and Alexandra and Annet were tested at 55 and 59 months of age.

Materials

We administered this test twice, in two separate tests of six trials each. A different set of six objects was used for each test. Each object had a sticker attached to one side of it. Figure 18 (a) and (b) presents a photograph of each of these two sets of objects.

Procedure

Chimpanzees were in their cage and two experimenters, E1 and E2, were outside the cage. Figure 19 presents a diagram of the testing situation. There were two experimental conditions, one in which the object was familiar to E1 and one in which it was new to E1. In the *Object Familiar* condition, E1 sat outside the enclosure facing the chimpanzee. She showed the chimpanzee one of the objects and they explored it together through the mesh for 50 seconds. E1 made sure that the side of the object with the sticker on it was also visible to chimpanzees occasionally, without ever calling attention to the sticker. E2 sat to the left of E1 and watched this play passively. After 50 seconds had elapsed, E1 stopped playing and walked over to the door, where she fiddled with the light switches. While E1 was there, E2 placed the toy in the middle of the room with the sticker side facing away from chimpanzees.

In the *Object New* condition, the procedure was very similar, except that instead of playing with the object with the chimpanzee, E1 left the room at the beginning of the trial, closing the door behind her, before the assigned object was brought out. While E1 was gone, E2 brought out the assigned object and explored it together with the chimpanzee for 50 seconds in a similar way to that used in the other condition. After 50 seconds had elapsed, E2 stopped playing and placed the toy in the middle of the room with the sticker side facing away from chimpanzees, after which E1 re-entered the room.

From this point on, the procedure was identical in the two conditions. E1 approached the object from the door area and faced the sticker side of it.

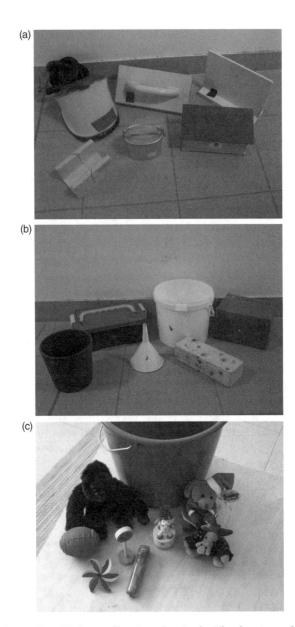

FIGURE 18.—Understanding Attention Study: The three sets of objects.

She said excitedly, "Oh, wow, look! [Name of chimpanzee], oh, look! Look!" looking back and forth from the object to the chimpanzee. (For the first set of objects she also made excited chimpanzee noises.) She did this for 1 minute, during which chimpanzees' responses were coded.

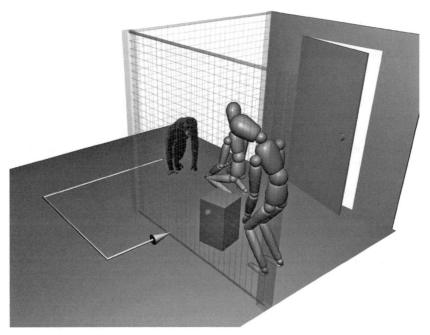

FIGURE 19.—Understanding Attention Study: The setup.

The first of the two tests consisted of three testing sessions: one per week, each with two trials, one in each condition (in the order Object-Familiar, Object-New), for a total of six trials. The second test took place 4 months later in a single session with all six trials alternating (beginning with Object-New). There were thus a total of 12 trials, 6 in each condition.

Coding and Reliability

The main measure of interest was whether chimpanzees moved around to look at E1's side of the object (the side with the sticker on it) during the minute that E1 was looking excitedly at the object. This response would be consistent with that of the older children in the Object Familiar condition of the Moll et al. (submitted) study, and would suggest that chimpanzees inferred that E1 could not be referring in such an excited way about something she had played with just a moment ago (and that they were looking to see what aspect of the object they had previously missed). Because chimpanzees moved around the cage a lot, and because the caging made it impossible always to see where, precisely, they were looking, we were only able to code whether or not chimpanzees visited the area of the cage close to the mesh where they would be able to see the sticker, and if so, how long they spent in this location. We also coded any "searching looks," that is, looks around the object or even around the testing area that suggested that chimpanzees were looking for another referent for E1's excitement besides the object as a whole.

Responses were coded from the videotapes. To assess interobserver reliability, 36% of the tapes were coded by an independent coder who was blind to condition. The coders agreed on 100% of trials whether the chimpanzee visited the area of the cage close to the mesh where they would be able to see the sticker. Their measurements of duration across trials correlated highly, $r = .99$, $n = 13$, $p < .0001$, and there was no significant difference between them, $t(12) = .56$, $p = .58$.

Follow-Up Study

Chimpanzees were tested once more approximately 3.5 months later (Alex was 45 months old and Alexandra and Annet were 63 months old) with a slightly different procedure, which enabled us to determine more easily when they looked at the object. Eight further objects and a bucket were used (see Figure 18c). Instead of investigating whether chimpanzees looked at the side of the object E was looking at in order to see some interesting aspect of it they might have missed, we investigated whether chimpanzees looked into a bucket that the object had been placed in, in order to see whether there might be something else there. Again, in the Object Familiar condition, E1 explored the object with chimpanzees (this time for 30 seconds), and then went over to the light switches. E2 then put the object in a bucket near the chimpanzees' enclosure. In the Object New condition, the same procedure was followed except that E1 left at the beginning of the trial and E2 explored the object with chimpanzees (also for 30 seconds). From that point on, the procedure was identical in each of these two conditions: E2 gave food or juice to chimpanzees to bring them back to a starting location on the floor, and then E1 returned and gave the same excited response as in the previous administrations of the test while leaning over and peering into the bucket (without making chimpanzee noises).

Coders scored from videotapes whether chimpanzees looked into the bucket. In order to get a score of looking, chimpanzees had to climb up and make a clear look down into the bucket from a position close to (within 1 m from) the Plexiglas panel in front of the bucket (this position was determined by a coder who entered the enclosure after the test and checked various locations to establish from where it was possible to see into the bucket). Coders also scored latency to chimpanzees' first look into the bucket. Interobserver reliability for looks was excellent: Cohen's $\kappa = .80$. For latency, there was a significant correlation between the two coders'

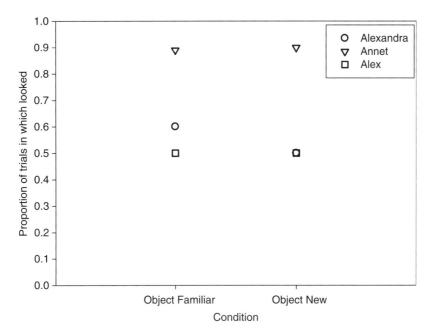

FIGURE 20.—Understanding Attention Study: The proportion of trials in which each chimpanzee went to a location where they could see the sticker side of the object.

scores, $r = .94$, $n = 16$, $p < .001$, and no significant difference between them, $t(15) = .52$, $p = .61$.

Results

Figure 20 shows the proportion of trials in which each of the three chimpanzees locomoted to a new location in order to see what E was looking at across the three test administrations combined (measured slightly differently in the three administrations). They looked to the location E looked an average of 66% of their trials in the Object Familiar condition, and 63% of their trials in the Object New condition—clearly no difference (no segregation of distributions). Similar negative results are also found when the duration of time spent in the proper location is used as a dependent measure (distributions in the two conditions do not segregate at all, with a trend in the "wrong" direction). Because we had better video angles and a slightly different procedure in the follow-up study, we also looked at that test separately, using the more stringent measure of looking to where E looked, but again there was no difference between conditions: two of the chimpanzees looked where E looked an equal proportion of times in the two conditions (.50 and 1.00), and one chimpanzee looked more often in the Object Familiar condition (.75) than in the Object New condition (.25). There was also

89

no difference between conditions in latency to look in this follow-up study: mean latencies were 12.64 and 12.41 seconds in the Object Familiar and Object New conditions, respectively.

Because human children in the study of Moll et al. (submitted) sometimes looked not to the side of the object, but rather to other places in the room (especially in the Object Familiar condition), also important are any "searching looks" chimpanzees might have performed to locations other than the target object. They performed none of these in either experimental condition.

Discussion

Although these chimpanzees could follow others' gaze and demonstrated an understanding that others could see things, these results provide no support for the hypothesis that young chimpanzees understand what is new and old in the experience of others, nor that they use such an understanding to determine where other individuals' attention is focused within their perceptual field. Human infants demonstrate such knowledge in the same task from around 14 months of age (Moll et al., submitted; see also Tomasello & Haberl, 2003).

In their analysis of 12-month-old infants' successful performance in a similar task, Tomasello and Haberl (2003) claimed that two fundamental social-cognitive skills are required. First, subjects have to know that people get excited about new things, not old things, and second, they have to know which object—or aspect of an object—is new for the experimenter in this particular situation. The first of these represents general knowledge of human behavior, whereas the second represents knowledge of whether someone has or has not experienced something in a particular situation. Together, infants use these two pieces of knowledge to determine where an adult's attention is focused. The current results do not enable us to determine which of these two skills (or perhaps others) chimpanzees may be lacking, relative to children, in this experimental situation.

Interestingly, one can look at this task as a kind of perceptual analog to the Gergely et al. (2002) rational imitation procedure. In that procedure, infants understand why someone has chosen the action they have in a particular situation having particular constraints: they assumed that the adult must have a reason for performing that unusual action. In the current study, too, to be successful subjects need to understand that the adult reacted excitedly for reason—a different reason depending on her prior experience with the object. The difference in this case, then, is that the underlying reason in the current study is more "mental" than physical. The important point is that in both studies the subject must understand something about why someone has chosen to act in a certain way or to focus their attention in a certain way—potentially based on a wide variety of factors both in that person's past history and in the environmental situation. Human infants are good in both of these at 14 months of age, whereas chimpanzees so far have demonstrated competence in neither. Whether this is an issue of competence, or motivation, or both, is still to be determined.

SUMMARY AND DISCUSSION

Once again, when we look across the three studies in this section, a relatively coherent picture emerges. Chimpanzees in the first two studies clearly understood something about others' visual perception. They followed others' gaze to hidden locations behind a barrier, and they used gestures to beg from a human most often when the human could see them (and was ready to comply). However, our three young chimpanzees showed no evidence of understanding that others can focus their attention selectively for some particular reason.

NOTE

5. Along with coding 'sure' looks to the place E had looked, we also coded whether or not chimpanzees visited the area of the cage where they would be able to see what E was looking at. Perfect interobserver agreement was achieved on this measure. A similar pattern of results was found. Chimpanzees visited this location on 63% of the experimental trials as compared with only 20% of the control trials. The distributions segregate totally, and there was a statistically reliable difference between them, $t(2) = 7.13, p = .019$. Because subjects had enough trials in each condition, it is possible to look at each individual's performance separately using Fisher's Exact Probability tests. Alexandra went to the appropriate location more in experimental than in the control trials, $p = .027$. Alex also went to the appropriate location more in experimental than in the control trials, $p = .009$. Although Annet's values were in the same direction, they did not differ significantly between the two conditions, $p = .121$.

V. JOINT INTENTIONS AND ATTENTION

Chimpanzees thus understand a good bit about others' goals (if not their intentions), and a good bit about others' perception (if not their attention). But to engage in the shared cooperative activities that result in human culture, this understanding is not enough. In addition, these understandings need to be combined with the skills and motivations for sharing intentions and attention (or goals and perception) with others. Thus, to acquire many of the basic skills of a culture—especially those that have a strong conventional component such as the conventional use of many symbols and artifacts—children must create with adults some kind of joint attentional frame within which the convention makes sense. And joint attentional frames are mostly the result of joint activities involving joint goals and intentions. For example, to acquire the appropriate conventional use of the novel word *modi*, a child must enter into a frame in which "we" are doing something together which determines where the adult's attention is focused, and where the adult wants the child's attention to be focused, in using this novel word.

In the next two studies we investigate different aspects of the ability and motivation to coordinate intentions and attention with others. First, we test a simple form of collaboration in which the experimenter offers an object to subjects for them to act on, and then sets up a situation encouraging the subjects to switch roles and offer the object back to her. Second, we test subjects' ability to collaborate with the experimenter communicatively in order to comprehend the communicative intentions behind gestures intended to inform subjects of the location of hidden food.

COLLABORATION WITH ROLE REVERSAL

Collaboration has two essential characteristics that most clearly distinguish it from more general forms of social interaction (Bratman, 1992). First, there is a shared goal in the sense that each participant has the goal that we (in mutual knowledge) do X together. Second, there are joint intentions with reciprocal roles that both participants know, in the sense that they coordinate their plans of action and intentions some way down the hierarchy with the possibility of reversing roles, and even helping the other with his role if needed. This form of collaboration suggests a particular kind of dialogic cognitive representation in which each participant represents the entire collaboration—its shared goal and reciprocal roles—holistically, from a bird's-eye view, as it were.

Human children collaborate with others in interactions showing both of these characteristics between about 12 and 18 months of age. Naturalistic observations consistent with this interpretation are reported by Ratner and Bruner (1978) and Ross and Lollis (1987), in which children are seen interacting in collaborative games adults involving complementary roles such as peekaboo and rolling a ball back and forth. By 18–24 months of age infants begin to engage with peers in complex collaborative activities involving turn-taking (Eckerman, 1996) and they also at this age begin to engage with peers in collaborative activities with clearly differentiated roles (Brownell & Carriger, 1990). Experimentally, in a current study from our laboratory, Warneken, Chen, and Tomasello (submitted) programmed an adult partner to quit acting at some point in a collaborative game with 18-month-olds. Every infant at least once actively encouraged the adult to rejoin the game, suggesting the possibility that the child understood that they had a joint goal, in which they wanted the adult to re-engage. In some of the tasks, the adult played one role in one round of the game, and then in the next round took the child's former role, "forcing" the child to take the adult's former role (which the child had only previously observed the adult playing). Again, almost all 18-month-olds did this at least once.

Carpenter, Tomasello, and Striano (in press) found that even some 12-month-olds can engage in role reversals. They set up situations in which an adult did things like hold out a basket in which the child should place a toy (or hid something for the child to find). After the child complied, the adult then placed the basket in front of the child and held the toy herself—being careful not to prompt the child in any specific way. Some 12- and 18-month-olds then took their turn by holding out the basket for the adult spontaneously and, importantly, looking to her face in anticipation of her placing something in it (or they hid the toy for the adult, looking to her face, in the other task). Every researcher from Bates (1979) to Camaioni (1993) has held that a look to the face is necessary for the child to be "offering." Carpenter et al. also tested children with autism, and found that, although they often held out the basket (or hid the toy), they did not look to the adult in the same way, perhaps suggesting that they were mimicking the adult's action without understanding that they were reversing roles and engaging in a collaborative interaction.

In the wild, chimpanzees engage in some interactions that look cooperative, as reviewed in the introduction, but in experiments there has never been a single demonstration of two nonhuman primates playing complementary roles in a single collaborative interaction. Mostly the studies have demonstrated that when playing parallel roles (for example, two individuals pulling two ropes attached to a heavy box with food on it), chimpanzees quickly learn that it is useless to pull when the other is not pulling and so wait for the other (Crawford, 1937; Chalmeau, 1994; Povinelli & O'Neill, 2000). There is no evidence that they spontaneously encourage others to perform their role, nor is there any evidence that they can reverse roles in such interactions.

The one study purporting to show this ability is that of Povinelli, Nelson, and Boysen (1992). They gave chimpanzees a cooperative task in which one member of a pair (the communicator) was supposed to indicate for the other (the operator) where some food was located and the other then provided access to the food for both—and then roles were switched. It was always a human playing one role, and chimpanzees were trained to criterion in their initial role. After the switch, one of the two chimpanzees who had first been trained as communicator played its new role as operator efficiently from the beginning. But this subject almost certainly came to the study knowing how to comprehend a human indicating gesture (this was not pretested, and this subject had had extensive experience with humans). Both of the two individuals who had initially been trained as operators and then switched to communicators learned to designate for the human the location of the food fairly quickly. But in this case it is not clear to what degree these subjects actually indicated anything for the human and to what degree the human was simply able to discern the location of the food from the chimpanzees' involuntary behaviors such as looking. This study thus does not provide unambiguous evidence for role reversal abilities in chimpanzees (see Tomasello & Call, 1997, for more details of this critique, and also for a critique of the study of Savage-Rumbaugh et al., 1978, who trained two chimpanzees extensively in both roles of a task before testing them).

In the current study, we used the Carpenter et al. (in press) procedure to see if the chimpanzees would reverse roles in a very simple collaborative games with a human experimenter.

Pilot Study

We began by trying informally the hiding/finding game from Carpenter et al. (in press). During the months before the age for the main role reversal study, a familiar social partner of the chimpanzees (the first author) hid an interesting object for chimpanzees under either a plastic bucket or a cardboard box. Chimpanzees found the object easily on almost every trial.

Then, to test role reversal, the human placed the object and the bucket/box in front of the chimpanzee and waited expectantly to see if they would hide the object for him. This was done five to ten times with Alexandra and Annet and several times with Alex. None of the chimpanzees ever reversed roles at all: they found objects we hid for them, but they never hid one for us in return—as human infants often do.

We therefore used only the offering/placing game, but the disadvantage here was that all three chimpanzees had previously been trained by humans to hand over objects upon request. It was thus crucial that as evidence of collaborative role reversal they did something to indicate that they were really offering, and not just responding to a perceived request. The clearest evidence of this for infants in the Carpenter et al. (in press) study was that they held out the object and looked to the adult's face in anticipation of her playing her role. We thus looked for the same such evidence in chimpanzees.

Method

Participants

Alex was tested at age 35 months and Alexandra and Annet were tested at age 53 months.

Materials

Four pairs of objects were used: a plastic "Tigger" figure and a plate, a stuffed pig and a small cup, a "Lego" block and a drinking cup, a plastic "Winnie the Pooh" figure and a wagon. See Figure 21 for photographs of each pair.

Procedure

The chimpanzee sat with a familiar caregiver on the floor. The experimenter, E, sat facing the chimpanzee and presented the chimpanzee with the first of four pairs of objects that fit together in various ways. One of each pair of objects was designated the "actor" and the other was the "base." E first put the objects together twice, without letting the chimpanzee touch them (e.g., she put the tiger on the plate twice—or more, until E thought chimpanzees understood the game). Then E gave the chimpanzee the actor (the tiger) and held out the base (the plate). E waited, looking at the chimpanzee without speaking, and then, if the chimpanzee did not respond by

FIGURE 21.—*Collaboration and Role Reversal Study*: The objects in their final state.

putting the actor in/on the base, E encouraged the chimpanzee to play by saying "hm . . . hm." If the chimpanzee still did not respond, E helped the chimpanzee put the actor with the base. E then detached the toys and repeated the sequence of holding out the base with encouragement if necessary.

To test for role reversal, E then gave the base to the chimpanzee, and held out the actor. Again E waited, looking at the chimpanzee without speaking, and then, if the chimpanzee did not respond by holding out the base, E encouraged the chimpanzee to play by saying "hm . . . hm." If the chimpanzee still did not respond, E helped the chimpanzee put the actor with the base. E then repeated this sequence with each of the remaining pairs of objects. Note that as compared with the infants' test in the Carpenter et al. (in press) study, in this test during the waiting period E was often more active, holding out the actor close to chimpanzees and shaking it, and enthusiastically encouraging the chimpanzee (because this seemed to be the only way to keep the chimpanzees engaged in the task). Chimpanzees thus had less chance to perform the role reversal spontaneously.

Coding and Reliability

We coded whether chimpanzees offered the base to E, and whether they did this spontaneously or with some encouragement or help.

Importantly, we also noted whether chimpanzees looked to E's face during their offer. Interobserver reliability was assessed for 100% of the trials. Cohen's κ's were 1.0 for offers, .54 for spontaneity (but the percent agreement here was 92%), and 1.0 for looks to E's face.

Results

Alexandra and Alex each held out the base toward E at some point during three of their four trials, and Annet did this on two of her four trials. However, in all of these cases, the base toy was given only after encouragement from the experimenter, and, more importantly, no individual ever looked to E while holding out the toy—a key criterion of offering used in all previous studies with human children. There were thus no clear offers of the base object in acts of role reversal.

We should also mention here that we also conducted a more systematic series of collaborative problem-solving tasks with these same three chimpanzees and human 18- and 24-month-olds in a separate study (Warneken, Chen, & Tomasello, submitted). In this study, there were four different tasks of various kinds, two of which potentially involved role reversal, and the human interactant stopped cooperating in the middle of the game as an additional diagnostic of what the chimpanzees understood of the interaction. The first result was that the chimpanzees apparently never attempted to re-engage the human's participation, as the human infants often seemed to do (each child at least once). The second result was that whereas there were some instances of the chimpanzee performing the human's action, these did not occur with looks to the partner (which they did for most of the human children) and so were not considered role reversal.

Discussion

The current results provide little support for the hypothesis that chimpanzees can reverse roles in a triadic activity with a human. Even though chimpanzees could imitate by this age (see results from Chapters 2 and 3), and indeed often held out the toy, they never did so in an offering way, with looks, to the experimenter. And to repeat, every researcher from Bates (1979) to Camaioni (1993) has held that a look to the face is necessary for the child to be "offering." Our confidence in this conclusion must be tempered, however, by two considerations. First, these three chimpanzees had been previously trained in giving objects to humans when they requested them, and this might have actually interfered with their performance in this task. Second, as noted above, a review of the videotapes showed that in some trials the experimenter did not wait so long for a chimpanzee response (mainly because otherwise the chimpanzee would have run away), and so chimpanzees perhaps did not have a full opportunity to respond spontaneously. Nevertheless, in the current study the chimpanzees did nothing—like looking to E—that would lead us to believe that they were reversing roles.

Importantly, in the study of Carpenter et al. (in press) using basically the same tasks as in the current study, 12- and 18-month-old human infants reversed roles with the adult on about one-third of all trials (often spontaneously—although the adult did to some extent organize the turn-taking sequences of the game), and they looked to the adult as they offered the support toy on almost two-thirds of those trials. It should be noted that the human infants performed the task with a stranger, and it seemed that in some cases the children were shy with this new person—and so the Carpenter et al. study may actually be underestimating their abilities. In contrast, the chimpanzees should not have had this problem as they were performing the task with a highly familiar human adult.

In the collaborative problem-solving tasks with these same three chimpanzees reported above (Warneken, Chen, & Tomasello, submitted) results suggested that none of our three individuals attempted to re-engage the interactant when he stopped interacting nor did they clearly reverse roles. In our interpretation, the reason the chimpanzees did not attempt to re-engage their interactant was because they had not formed with him a shared goal, and the reason they did not reverse roles was because they had not formed with him any joint intentions involving complementary roles in the interaction.

Our overall conclusion, then—based on the current experiment in combination with previous and other research—is simply that chimpanzees do not engage in the kind of collaborative interactions in which they understand the collaboration from a "bird's-eye view" in which there is a joint goal and both roles are in the same representational format, and so easily reversed as needed (Tomasello, 1999).

UNDERSTANDING COMMUNICATIVE INTENTIONS

Human symbolic communication is inherently collaborative (Clark, 1996). As human beings converse with one another they are playing the complementary roles of speaker and listener, and each is doing his part toward the common goal of the listener comprehending the speaker's communicative intention. Said another way, the joint goal of speaker and listener is to reorient the listener's intentions and attention so that they align with those of the speaker, and their complementary roles (joint intentions) serve to do this through various kinds of collaborative communicative acts. Thus, the speaker collaborates by expressing his communicative intentions in ways that are potentially comprehensible by the listener, even clarifying (helping) when necessary; and the listener collaborates by making good-faith attempts at comprehension by following the speaker's attention-directing signals, making appropriate and relevant inferences, and asking for clarification (help) when needed. These two roles are actually directly embodied in the main conventional devices that human beings have created for purposes of communication, linguistic symbols, which are bi-directional in the sense that both speaker and listener know that the other could, if needed, play the other role (Saussure, 1916). Learning the conventional use of symbols thus involves role reversal imitation (using symbols toward others the way they have used them toward me), and it also involves taking shared perspectives on things and learning that people can choose to attend to things and to construe them in many different ways as needed (Clark, 1997; Tomasello, 1999).

From around 1 year of age human infants converse with adults in various ways, some involving a back-and-forth "negotiation of meaning" similar to that which goes on in mature conversation (Golinkoff, 1993). Within months of the first birthday, most infants have acquired the productive use of some bi-directional linguistic symbols for coordinating their actions and attention with others. Importantly, to comprehend and acquire any conventional communicative symbol—even nonlinguistic ones such as the pointing gesture—infants must construct with adults some shared frame of reference (common ground, joint attentional frame). For example, suppose that a person meets a friend on the street who points toward a building. What does she intend by this? The answer is that one cannot tell, if she and the friend do not share some frame of reference that grounds this deictic gesture in something common to them. Thus, if they share the knowledge that the first person is looking for her dentist's office, then the point is immediately and effortlessly meaningful.

Human infants begin to construct such joint attentional frames with adults, as shared frames of reference for their communicative interactions, from soon after the first birthday (Bakeman & Adamson, 1984). Behne, Carpenter, and Tomasello (in press) explored how 14-month-old and older infants use such frames to read the communicative intentions of an adult as expressed in a pointing gesture. An experimenter and infant played a hiding/finding game in which the experimenter hid a toy in one of two opaque buckets and then encouraged the infant to find it. Initially, the experimenter actually lifted the bucket and showed the infant where it was. But then in later trials the experimenter only pointed to the toy's hidden location. In this case, the infant not only had to follow the direction of the experimenter's point to the bucket, but also had to infer the relevance of this gesture to their shared goal that the infant find the toy. Without some understanding of this shared goal, the point—as in the example of the friends meeting on the street—would be meaningless. The infant had to see the "relevance" of the pointing gesture to the current joint intentional and attentional frame (Sperber & Wilson, 1986) in order to understand that in gesturing the experimenter was attempting to inform the infant of the toy's location. It is interesting to note that infants did this only when the experimenter pointed in an ostensive-communicative way, and not in a Control condition in which the experimenter extended her index finger while looking down at her watch instead of at the infant. This thus rules out associative learning explanations for the infants' findings.

Though seemingly simple and transparent, this process of interpreting a pointing gesture is not a foregone conclusion (as first noted by Wittgenstein, 1955). For example, otherwise bright and attentive chimpanzees and other apes perform very poorly in this "simple" task, no matter what kind of communicative cue is used (see Call & Tomasello, in press, for a review of many studies). The problem is not that apes cannot follow the direction of the human's point (with gaze) to the target location, which they easily can do. The problem is that when they follow the point to the opaque bucket, they do not know what it means. Because they have not constructed with the human a collaborative hiding/finding game with a shared goal and complementary roles (joint intentions), the pointing gesture is not seen as relevant to their own individual goal of finding the prize—which, from their perspective, the experimenter has nothing to do with. And chimpanzees' performance in this task is not inconsistent with the nature of their vocal and gestural communication with one another in more natural settings—which is clearly not collaborative in the same way as human communication. Chimpanzees do not really engage in cooperative conversation, their communicative signals are not really bidirectional, and they do not ever spontaneously point to things or show things to one another just to inform them or share interest (Tomasello, 1998).

In the current study, we used the hiding/finding game of Behne et al. (in press)—one variant of the object choice procedure—to see if perhaps our chimpanzees, who had had much communicative interaction with humans who pointed for them often and showed them things regularly, might be able to succeed in this task where other apes have not. From the longitudinal study, we knew that all three of these chimpanzees already could follow others' points (and they also could perform some communicative gestures themselves). Here, we tested whether they could go beyond point following and also infer the relevance of others' gestures to a shared goal.

Method

Participants

Alex was tested at age 40 months and Alexandra and Annet were tested at age 59 months.

Materials

Two identical inverted plastic cups were used as hiding places. A sponge was used as a marker. Small pieces of fruit were used as rewards. An opaque occluder (a 31 × 73 cm black plastic screen attached to a wooden stand) was used to screen the hiding process. Attached to the outside of chimpanzees' enclosure was a 38 × 82 cm platform on which a 27 × 80 cm plastic tray rested on two metal tracks, which allowed E to slide the tray back and forth from herself to adjacent to the chimpanzees' enclosure (see Figure 22). A vertical Plexiglas panel with three holes (each 3.7 cm diameter) in it was

FIGURE 22.—*Understanding Communicative Intentions Study*: Each of the two cues from the chimpanzees' perspective. (a) Point, (b) Marker.

101

RETA E. KING LIBRARY
CHADRON STATE COLLEGE
CHADRON NE

set into the mesh at this location. When the tray was slid forward to the chimpanzees' enclosure, chimpanzees could stick their fingers through the holes to choose a container.

Procedure

The experimenter, E, sat outside the enclosure facing the chimpanzee sitting inside through a large Plexiglas window. E began with a warm-up procedure with visible hiding designed to introduce chimpanzees to the general procedure. In the warm-up procedure, E placed the two cups on the tray on her side of the platform, aligned with the two holes in the Plexiglas. She concealed the cups from the chimpanzee with the occluder, showed the chimpanzee a piece of food above the occluder, and then removed the occluder and hid the food visibly under one of the cups. E waited 5 seconds, then pushed the tray forward for the chimpanzee to choose a cup by sticking a finger through the corresponding hole in the Plexiglas. E gave chimpanzees the food if they chose correctly; if not, E showed them where the food was but put it away without giving it to them. Chimpanzees had to meet a criterion of four correct choices in a row before moving on to the test trials.

For test trials, the general procedure was the same, with the important exception that the hiding process was concealed by the occluder so chimpanzees did not know where the food was. There were two experimental conditions, Point and Marker, in which E provided a communicative cue as to where the food was for chimpanzees, and a Control condition in which E did not indicate the location of the food, as follows. After hiding the food and removing the occluder, in the Point condition, E gestured for the chimpanzee with an extended index finger to the correct cup, alternating her gaze back and forth between the chimpanzee and the cup silently for 5 seconds. The point was held in the middle of E's body, at an equal distance to each cup. E then stopped pointing and pushed the tray forward for chimpanzees' choice. In the Marker condition, after hiding the food and removing the occluder, E placed the sponge onto the correct cup for the chimpanzee, alternating her gaze back and forth between the chimpanzee and the cup silently for 5 seconds. E moved the marker to the cup across her body. She left the marker on the cup until chimpanzees had made their choice. If chimpanzees did not watch the cues, E called their names. Figure 22 shows each of the two cues from the chimpanzees' perspective.

In a third condition, the Control condition, E provided no communicative cues. After hiding the food and removing the occluder, E sat still, looking straight ahead silently for 5 seconds, then pushed the tray forward for chimpanzees' choice. In all conditions, when chimpanzees chose correctly, E gave them the food; when chimpanzees did not choose correctly, E showed them where the food was but then went on to the next trial without giving it to them.

In each of the three conditions there were 18 trials. Conditions were administered in blocks, one block per day, on 3 consecutive days. For Alexandra and Annet, the order of conditions was Point, Control, Marker, and for Alex it was Marker, Control, Point. The hiding place was determined in advance randomly, but food was never hidden more than twice in a row in the same location.

Scoring

E, who was blind to the hypotheses of the study, coded all trials live, and then checked them afterward using the videotape. Chimpanzees' choice was scored as the first hole they stuck a finger through after the tray was pushed forward. On a total of 13 trials (four for Annet, six for Alexandra, and three for Alex; 12 in the Point and Marker conditions), E could not determine with certainty which cup the chimpanzees had chosen, because they stuck their finger through a different, middle hole in the Plexiglas or else moved quickly back and forth between the left and right holes. These trials were replaced by extra trials at the end of the session. Otherwise, choices were unambiguous and so, following standard procedure in object choice tests (e.g., Call, Agnetta, & Tomasello, 1998), interobserver reliability was not specifically assessed.

Results

Figure 23 presents the number of times (out of 18) each of the three chimpanzees chose the correct container in each condition of this object choice task. Neither of the two experimental conditions with communicative cues—Point or Marker—differed from (segregated from) the Control condition with no cue and neither segregated from the Control condition distributionally.

However, for the Marker versus Control comparison, there was a reasonably large numerical advantage for the Marker condition. The individual probabilities, as assessed by Fischer's exact tests for each individual, were:

Alexandra:	$p = .99$
Annet:	$p = .06$
Alex:	$p = .49$

Using the Rosenthal (1991) procedure, this leads to a combined probability of .15, which does not enable us to reject the null hypothesis of no difference between conditions.

103

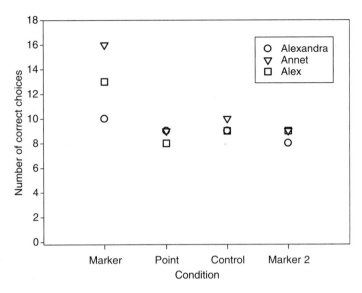

FIGURE 23.—*Understanding Communicative Intentions Study*: Number of times (out of 18) each subject chose the correct container.

Follow-Up Study

Chimpanzees showed no comprehension of E's communicative intention when pointing was the cue E used. In contrast, chimpanzees' (especially Annet's) responses in the Marker condition were not clearly negative. However, based on previous studies and on chimpanzees' behavior, we were afraid that chimpanzees might have actually been interested in the sponge and were reaching for the marker on top of the bucket in the Marker condition in order to obtain it, rather than indicating their choice of a container. We therefore re-ran this condition again, this time removing the marker before the chimpanzee's choice.

Chimpanzees were thus tested on 18 trials of the Marker 2 condition 2–4 weeks after the initial test. The procedure was identical to that of the Marker procedure, except that after placing the sponge, E waited 3–4 seconds, then removed the sponge (placing it in her lap, out of sight), and then pushed the tray forward for chimpanzees' choice. Results for the Marker 2 condition are also presented in Figure 23. It can be seen that in this condition—administered after chimpanzees had been mostly successful in the Marker condition—all three chimpanzees returned to chance performance.

Discussion

The three young chimpanzees in this study performed very much like other chimpanzees previously tested in this experimental paradigm.

104

Although there are some exceptions, for the most part chimpanzees do not seem to understand this task as a collaborative one, in which the human is doing various things to indicate for them the location of the hidden food (see Call & Tomasello, in press, for a review). Various explanations are possible, but our preferred explanation is that chimpanzee social interaction never takes on the kind of collaborative structure characteristic of human social interaction. In this task, therefore, chimpanzees do not form with the human experimenter a joint goal and joint intentions for achieving that goal, which would make the pointing gesture and marker immediately relevant for the task of finding the food. Motivationally, informing someone about the location of food that could be retained for the self—in a helpful, cooperative way—is not something that chimpanzees regularly do or experience in their normal lives.

In contrast, as noted above, human infants are successful in this task at 14–18 months of age. They construct with the adult a shared game of hiding/finding—with a shared goal and joint intentions—within which understanding of the communicative cue is straightforward, and they understand from their daily lives that people sometimes help one another by informing them of things they need to know (and they themselves help others in this way by age 12 months; Liszkowski et al., in press). To the degree that chimpanzees may in some cases become successful in this task, our hypothesis would be that they are in all cases using alternative strategies (such as reaching for the marker in our Marker 1 condition or learning a discriminative cue). The current study shows that even when they are raised mostly by humans, chimpanzees do not fully understand human-style communicative intentions as they are expressed within the context of shared goals, joint intentions, and joint attention. We should also note, for perspective, that when chimpanzees are administered a competitive version of this task involving a competitive human reaching for the bucket containing the hidden food (not trying to show them anything), they are suddenly successful (Hare & Tomasello, 2004).

SUMMARY AND DISCUSSION

Once again, we have a fairly clear picture of our three chimpanzees' skills in this domain. Although we administered only two tasks, both are seemingly very simple. In the first case, to be successful all the chimpanzee had to do was hold out an object expectantly, offering it to the human—having just seen the human do it for them. But they did not do this. In the second case, all they had to do was follow the human's pointing gesture, or physical marker, to find the location of hidden food that they wanted very much. But again they did not. Although we clearly do not know all of the parameters here, and other explanations are possible (e.g., as always in experiments, we may not have tested their skills appropriately), we believe that these two failures (and many other similar failures in other experiments) are best explained by positing that chimpanzees do not construct with others—either conspecifics or humans—the kinds of collaborative activities with shared goals and joint intentions that are the daily staff of human infants' social and communicative interactions with adults from soon after their first birthday.

VI. GENERAL DISCUSSION

Obviously one must be cautious in making generalizations to an entire species from three individuals, each of whom has its own individual history. Nevertheless, we believe that the results we have reported here are basically reliable and reflect accurately the social-cognitive skills of the species as a whole, most especially those who have had extensive human contact. The reason for our "cautious optimism" is that for each of the basic skills we investigated (e.g., understanding intentions, understanding perception, collaborating) we had more than one task, each with more than one administration, and, generally speaking, tasks requiring the same kind of understanding gave us the same results. In addition and just as importantly, the current results in most cases fit quite closely with previous findings with apes for each of the different skills—although in some cases we did new things that no one else had done precisely (e.g., rational plans and attention), in which case we must be more cautious about the results. And although, as is well known, negative results present special problems of interpretation, in the case of apes' lack of skills of joint intentions and attention (collaboration) we again have several findings that all tell the same story and agree in general outline with previous research.

SUMMARY OF RESULTS

Although, to repeat, each of the particular results reported here must be assessed with caution—both because there were only three individuals and because these three individuals have somewhat special histories—in general our longitudinal and experimental results together paint a fairly clear picture. As summarized in Table 3, with respect to the understanding of intentional action, our three juvenile chimpanzees behaved like human infants in reproducing the goal an actor intended, not the result the actor actually caused in the environment, in both the Failed Attempts and Accident studies. This finding is supported in general by: (1) Tomasello,

107

TABLE 3

SUMMARY OF RESULTS OF THE EXPERIMENTS

Understanding Intentional Action		Understanding Perception/ Attention		Joint Intentions/Attention	
Failed attempts	Yes	Gaze following barriers	Yes	Role reversal	—
Accidents	Yes	Perceptual mechanisms	Yes	Understanding	—
Copy style	—	Understanding attention	—	communicative intentions	
Rational plans	—				

Carpenter, Call, Behne, and Moll (1993), who found human-like skills of imitative learning in three other human-raised apes (see also Russon & Galdikas, 1993; Bering, Bjorklund, & Ragan, 2000; Bjorklund, Bering, & Ragan, 2000, for similar findings with human-raised orangutans), and (2) findings using other methodologies suggesting an understanding of goals (e.g., Call, Hare, Carpenter, & Tomasello, 2004). Unlike human infants in previous studies, however, the chimpanzees did not also pay attention to the actual actions they saw: in the Copy Style study they reproduced the outcome they observed but not the action style of the actor (in none of the three task administrations). And unlike human infants chimpanzees did not pay attention to the reason why the actor chose the behavioral means that he did: in the Rational Plans study (in both administrations) they used the tool they saw the actor using equally often under all conditions. In general, findings over the past few decades have established that chimpanzees typically do not pay attention to an actor's actions when performing an instrumental behavior to nearly the same degree that human children do (although they can sometimes be trained to do so; see Tomasello, 1996; Whiten, Horner, Litchfield, & Marshall-Pescini, 2004, for reviews). Our young apes, who had had much human contact but no deliberate training in imitation, are no exception.

With regard to the understanding of perception and attention, a somewhat similar picture emerges. Again as can be seen in Table 3, like human infants the three juvenile chimpanzees followed the human's gaze to an out-of-sight location behind a barrier in the Barrier study, and they also adjusted their gestures and attention-getting attempts in most cases to take account of where the human was looking in the Mechanisms of Perception study (and they followed gaze in the longitudinal study). These are findings that accord with previous studies such as Bräuer, Call, and Tomasello (in press) and Kaminski, Call, and Tomasello (2004). But the chimpanzees were not attuned to the human's focus of attention within his visual field in the Understanding Attention study (in any of the three task administrations with slight variations)—which required them as a prerequisite to determine what was new for the adult in the situation. Other chimpanzees have also shown skills in following the gaze direction of others, and indeed in knowing what others see (see Call & Tomasello, in press, for a review), but there are no studies with any chimpanzees demonstrating an understanding of attention as it was defined and measured here. And so again our young human-raised apes are no exception to the more general findings in the experimental literature—although we establish the existence of these skills at younger ages than previous studies and the negative results give us more confidence in previous negative results.

The reason we say these two sets of findings are "similar" is the following. In our theoretical analysis, both intentional actions and perceptions are hierarchically organized. When a chimpanzee observes an actor opening a box successfully, for example, the inference is that the main goal of the action was indeed to open the box. When a chimpanzee observes an actor looking at, or even behind, a box, the inference is that the actor sees the box or what is behind it. But the Rational Plans and Understanding Attention studies require an understanding that in doing these things the actor is making choices. In the first instance, the actor has chosen one behavioral means rather than another for some reason—in our study having to do with environmental constraints—and in the second instance the actor has chosen to pay attention to one thing rather than to others for some reason as well—in our study having to do with the newness of some item in the perceptual field (a sort of psychological constraint). Understanding rational choice, either in the behavioral or perceptual domain, requires an analysis that goes beneath what actors want (their goal) and what they see to determine why they are doing what they are doing in pursuit of the goal and why they are attending to some things but not to others. One could argue that these are the most mental, and least observable, aspects of intentional action.

In our two tests investigating different types of collaborative interaction, also in Table 3, our three juvenile chimpanzees did not behave at all like human infants. In the Role Reversal task, we did not observe a single instance in which a chimpanzee offered a base-object back to the human the way the human had offered it to the chimpanzee, looking to the human while doing so—the way human infants often do from soon after the first birthday. Those instances in which chimpanzees did give the base-object, without looking, were very likely instances of their "give over" behavior which had been previously trained. We used this test because there is no question that chimpanzees can coordinate their behavior with others in various more or less complex ways, as, for example, in their cooperative hunting in the wild or in their rope-pulling behavior in experiments requiring coordinated action. The question is whether they understand collaborative interactions holistically, from a bird's-eye view, which implies a common representational format for both roles of the collaboration, leading naturally to the ability to reverse roles when necessary. The answer for the moment would seem to be negative, and this is reinforced by the study of Warneken, Chen, and Tomasello (submitted), briefly described above, in which these same three chimpanzees were not particularly collaborative as they participated in a more systematic series of cooperative problem-solving tasks—they neither attempted to re-engage a recalcitrant partner nor switched roles readily.

In the Communicative Intentions task—which we conceptualized as another type of collaborative task—the chimpanzees showed basically no ability to comprehend the human pointing gesture, or the use of a novel marker, to indicate the location of hidden food. This is consistent with the performance of virtually all apes who have been tested in this task previously in approximately a dozen experiments (with a few individual exceptions; see Call & Tomasello, in press, for a review). This is despite the fact that these human-raised individuals: (1) readily follow pointing and gaze to visible targets (see results of the longitudinal study), and (2) had experienced humans directing their attention by pointing many times on a daily basis for many months prior to this study. How could they follow pointing, but not know what it means? The answer, in our view, is that understanding the pointing gesture—even though it is not normally thought of in this way—is actually part of a collaborative act. Human symbolic communication, in which the pointing gesture plays an important role, requires that the signaler and the recipient construct some kind of shared joint attentional format (common ground) within which the directing of attention has a larger meaning (e.g., in the current experiment, the hiding/finding game). The human infants who do well in this task have constructed with the adult a shared hiding/finding game before the adult ever points, and so when the adult does point it is immediately meaningful within that collaborative and joint attentional format: I am searching and she is helping me, so the pointing act must be relevant to these roles. Our hypothesis is that the chimpanzees do not understand the communicative intentions behind the pointing gesture in this or other tasks precisely because they have not constructed with their partner such a shared joint attentional format, and so they follow the point to the opaque container but do not find it relevant to their search for food. It is as if they say to themselves: "OK, so there's the bucket. So what? Boring. Now where's the food?"

On the production side, it is also noteworthy that in our longitudinal study we did not observe a single instance of a truly joint attentional interaction between a chimpanzee and human, nor a single instance of a declarative gesture by a chimpanzee designed to share attention with another. We know of no observations anywhere with strong evidence for these skills in apes, and indeed in the most systematic investigation to date important differences in the way apes engage with humans were found (Carpenter, Tomasello, & Savage-Rumbaugh, 1995).

And so in broad outline and with appropriate caution the overall results of these studies support our predictions based on previous research and our new theoretical proposal. Chimpanzees understand that other individuals have goals and see things. But they do not engage with other individuals collaboratively, if collaboration is defined in terms of shared intentionality as forming with others shared goals and joint intentions for achieving those goals. Joint attention corresponds to the (inter)subjective aspect of collaborative activities involving the creation of a shared focus of attention on some third entity related to the shared goals or intentions.

Results from the Rational Plans and Understanding Attention studies suggest that chimpanzees do not understand that others pursue goals with rationally chosen means or choose to attend to things relevant to their goals and intentions. Assuming that these negative results are reliable and generalizable—which, given that these are the only studies of their kind, is something still to be established—a major question is whether there is any relation between chimpanzees' inabilities in these "understanding rational choice" tasks and their lack of collaborative interactions involving shared goals, joint intentions, and joint attention. We have no answer to this question at this time, but we will raise it again below in the context of human ontogeny and phylogeny and offer some speculations.

CHIMPANZEE COGNITIVE ONTOGENY AND ENCULTURATION

Contrary to our previous hypotheses (e.g., Tomasello, 1999), then, it now seems clear that chimpanzees understand important aspects of goal-directed action and perception. However, there is currently no evidence that they understand such things as beliefs, and indeed several indications that they do not (e.g., Call & Tomasello, 1999). The question of chimpanzee social cognition should therefore not be phrased as whether chimpanzees do or do not have a "theory of mind," but rather how chimpanzees understand the other social beings that make up their social worlds in all of their many dimensions.

In this connection, the current negative findings in the two experiments on the understanding of others' rational choices (Rational Plans and Understanding Attention) are interesting in yet another way. The original hypothesis of Tomasello and Call (1997) was that chimpanzees and other nonhuman primates do not understand unobservable causes in either the physical or social domain. The goals and visual perception of others are an important part of the causality/intentionality of their actions, and in an important sense they are not observable. But they do at least have some fairly consistent manifestations in overt behavior. Goals are at least indirectly indicated by such things as direction of action and perception, repetition and adjustment of behavioral means, and reaction to outcome. Perceptions are at least indirectly indicated by the direction in which the looker is looking. On the other hand, thoughts and beliefs have very few consistent behavioral manifestations at all. The process of making rational decisions in the context of intentional action and perception would seem to be somewhere in between—various ways of overcoming physical obstacles, signs of effort, taking another look, pausing, vocalizing "Hmm," and the like, may indirectly indicate the decision-making process, although not really its rational dimension. And so it is perhaps possible that the general idea of Tomasello and Call was correct, but that the line was simply drawn in the wrong place. Perhaps along the lines of Gergely and Csibra (2003), we may posit that all primates naturally perceive and understand the basics of goal-directed action and perception based on consistent observable accompaniments and indications, but that this does not extend to decision-making processes whereby an actor chooses a behavioral means or chooses to attend to only some aspects of a scene—much less to the realm of beliefs which have few if any consistent manifestations in overt behavior. On a somewhat deeper level, it is also possible that nonhuman primates are simply not able to cognitively represent multiple possible states of affairs simultaneously, or to understand the reason why actors choose one behavioral means over another.

It is possible, however, that our chimpanzees were just too young to understand these things. Even though human infants at around 14 months of age seem to understand rational choices in both action and attention, perhaps chimpanzees only come to understand these things at an older age—a possibility reinforced by findings of Boesch and Boesch-Achermann (2000), among others, who note that some forms of tool use in wild chimpanzees take many years to develop. Obviously we have no way of testing that hypothesis here. But in the opposite direction, it is also possible that our human-raised chimpanzees are showing more skills than would chimpanzees raised in a more species-typical environment, whatever their age. Based on the available data at the time, which seemed to show superior skills for human-raised ("enculturated") apes, Call and Tomasello (1996) hypothesized that perhaps being raised by humans in a human-like cultural environment actually created skills for understanding others as intentional agents—as only when they are raised by humans are they themselves treated as intentional agents whom others show things to and teach. But various lines of new data—as reviewed in the introduction—have convinced us that apes who grow up in all kinds of environments come to understand that others have goals and perceptions. So the original enculturation hypothesis is surely not correct.

112

In light of our results, it might still be possible to hold a weakened version of the enculturation hypothesis. For example, one might simply maintain that in growing up with humans who control their world and who interact with them in ways that other apes do not—for instance, attempting to direct their attention, comprehending their indicating gestures, requesting that they do things, teaching them things—apes become both more competent and more motivated to pay attention to the things that humans do and ask them to do. However, on the whole, even though our chimpanzees are still rather young, the current study does not provide strong support for the idea that growing up with humans fundamentally changes the nature of ape social cognition. Both enculturated and nonenculturated chimpanzees seem to understand others' goals and perceptions. But neither enculturated nor nonenculturated chimpanzees seem equipped to participate with others in collaborative acts involving joint intentions and attention; this seems to be a genuine species difference that no amount of cross-fostering can change fundamentally (Tomasello & Call, 2004).

Our results thus support the following general view of chimpanzee social-cognitive ontogeny. The developmental pathway for understanding intentional action and perception is not so different from the human version, although it may take a bit longer and it may not include an understanding of the rational dimensions of action and attention. But there does not seem to be anything in chimpanzee ontogeny comparable with the human developmental pathway for sharing and collaborating with others, that is, for engaging with others in protoconversations, declarative communication, and complex collaborative activities involving joint intentions and attention.

But we must also be sensitive to possible individual differences in this general pattern. Although again we have only three individuals, to briefly investigate possible individual differences among our three subjects, we ranked each of the three individuals on each of the nine experimental tasks (using tied ranks where appropriate). Recall that Alex was, on average, about 1.5 years younger than the other two when most of the tasks were administered, but he also differed in having had much more human experience than the other two (continuous since birth) and in the fact that he was male. Averaging the nine ranks for each individual we get the following figures (lower ranks are better): the average rank for Alexandra = 2.05, for Annet = 2.17, and for Alex = 1.78. There are obviously not great differences among these (t-tests using the nine tasks as subjects revealed no significant differences in any of the three possible pair-wise comparisons between individuals), but any advantage there is was for the youngest but most human-experienced subject Alex. In terms of specific tasks, Alexandra seemed to be especially skillful in tasks involving understanding perception, whereas Annet and Alex were especially skillful in tasks involving the understanding of goal-directed actions.

The current results potentially have important implications for our understanding of human cognitive ontogeny. Specifically, Tomasello et al. (in press) proposed that we should think of the development of human social-cognitive skills as comprising two intertwined ontogenetic strands: (1) the understanding of intentional action and perception, and (2) the propensity to understand and participate in shared social interactions involving one or another form of shared intentionality. The findings of the current studies bear on this hypothesis in a number of different ways.

The first strand of human social-cognitive ontogeny is the general primate (or perhaps only great ape) understanding of intentional action. Based on the current results as well as recent studies with other primate species we may propose that all primates understand individual intentional action in terms of the pursuit of goals, as well as the basics of visual perception. It is not clear from the current data exactly when this first emerges in chimpanzees (at least by the middle of the second year), but in human infants this line begins in earnest at around 9 months of age, as is widely recognized. There have been a number of proposals to the effect that this skill is a hard-wired and modular part of the human perceptual system. Just as humans automatically see certain perceptual sequences as causal (Michotte, 1963; Leslie, 1984), they automatically see certain actions performed by animate agents as goal directed. Gergely and Csibra (2003), for example, have proposed that human infants possess an action interpretation system that perceives human-like action as teleologically directed to a goal from the second half of the first year of life; independently developing is a reference interpretation system concerned with following gaze and the like (Csibra, 2003). Baron-Cohen (1995) proposes something similar, with two early developing innate modules involving the perceiving of goals and eye gaze direction. Soon after the first birthday an independent "shared attention mechanism," emerges, taking outputs from the two earlier modules as inputs.

Although our view shares some features with these views, there are two important differences. First, we do not see infants' understanding of goals/ intentions and perception/attention as blocked off from one another in a modular fashion. Indeed, much recent evidence on infant social-cognitive development suggests that in attempting to understand what others are doing and why they are doing it, infants comprehend intentional action and perception as an integrated system (i.e., as a kind of control system). They display such an integrated understanding perhaps as early as 9 months of age when they know that actors pursue goals persistently (until they perceive that the world matches their goal) and also when they engage with other persons triadically around external objects—where they infer people's perceptions from their goals and their goals from their perceptions.

In general, we do not see how an observer can understand goal-directed action (much less rational action) without conceiving a perceiving organism who monitors the world for signs of success, failure, obstacles, and so forth.

Second, we believe that to understand the origins of a human cognitive skill we must go beyond simply labeling it as "innate." Indeed, although we concur that understanding actions as goal directed is a biological adaptation, this says nothing about the ontogenetic process. It is very unlikely, in our view, that a human or ape kept in social isolation for the first year of life would suddenly understand others as goal-directed or intentional agents on its initial encounter with them; presumably the developmental pathway for understanding intentional action depends on species-typical social interactions early in ontogeny. This does not necessarily mean, however, any specific experiences. Thus, Kaye (1982) proposed that to understand intentions infants must themselves be treated by adults as intentional, in the sense that adults interpret their actions in adult-like terms and provide various types of feedback to this effect. The problem with this more specific hypothesis is that there seems to be fairly wide cultural variation in how infants are treated by adults—with adults in some cultures not really treating infants as fully intentional (Scheffelin & Ochs, 1986)—and, by all accounts, all children in all cultures develop an understanding of others as intentional agents.

The second strand is the sharing line of development. Theorists such as Trevarthen (1979), Stern (1985), Braten (2000), and especially Hobson (2002), have elaborated the interpersonal and emotional dimensions of early human ontogeny in great detail. We mostly agree with their accounts, but we find that they do not give sufficient attention to the other, intention-reading, line of social-cognitive development. Our proposal is that the uniquely human aspects of social cognition emerge only as uniquely human social motivations interact with an emerging, primate-general understanding of animate and goal-directed action—which then transforms the general ape line of understanding intentional action into the modern human line of shared intentionality.

Although the precise nature of this interaction is not entirely clear, our general view is that infants begin to understand particular kinds of intentional and mental states in others only after they have experienced them first in their own activity and then used their own experience to simulate that of others (Tomasello, 1999; see Sommerville & Woodward, 2005, for experimental evidence supporting this view). However, contrary to our previous view, we do not think that simple "identification with others" is a sufficient basis for the simulation process—certainly not if we mean bodily identification, as there is now evidence that neonatal chimpanzees engage in the same kind of facial mimicking as human infants (Myowa, 1996; Myowa-yamakoshi, Tomonaga, Tanaka, & Matsuzawa, 2004), and even some species of birds are good at copying actions (e.g., Zentall, 1996). And so we would speculate at this point that a more deeply psychological level of identification with others is part and parcel of the uniquely human skills and motivations for dyadic emotion sharing characteristic of young human infants and their caregivers (Hobson, 2002).

Again one can imagine that a species-typical social environment, involving human-typical social interactions with other persons, is required for the emergence of the sharing motivation and its related skills of social engagement. But again some theorists have proposed that some kinds of specific experiences are necessary. For instance, Stern (1985) proposes that parents must "mirror" back to infants their own emotions or behaviors and Gergely (2003) posits an especially important role for certain kinds of social contingencies in terms of timing. But again it is not clear that children in all cultures receive such experiences, or that children who are deprived of them end up unable to share psychological states with others (Scheffelin & Ochs, 1986)—and of course children with autism never learn to share psychological states with others in the normal fashion, despite their usually rich social environments. And so the ontogenetic process for sharing emotions and intentions with others may be fairly robust in the face of different particular human social environments.

Our proposal for the early developmental pathway characteristic of human social cognition is thus that it is the synergistic product of the general ape line of understanding intentional action, unfolding from 9 to 14 months (based on earlier recognition of object-directed actions), and the modern human motivation to share psychological states with others, present from very early in human ontogeny. There is almost no research establishing a solid relationship between any kind of particular social experience infants might have and individual differences in the unfolding of either of these developmental pathways. In the absence of such studies, we might tentatively conclude that both are very robust, heavily canalized ontogenetic pathways in humans that emerge in all "normal" human environments.

What results from the confluence of these two lines of development, early in the second year of life, is the ability to engage in a number of different kinds of collaborative interactions involving shared intentionality (joint intentions and attention). As a part of this, there also emerges a new form of cognitive representation, dialogic cognitive representations, in which each participant conceives the collaboration holistically, with both roles in a single representational format (Tomasello et al., in press; see Carpendale & Lewis, 2004, for a different view). Although we have no concrete evidence for where these novel forms of cognitive representation come from, our supposition is that they are Vygotskian internalizations of the various forms of psychological sharing in which infants and adults engage. These representations then enable children's participation in

116

collaborative cultural (mediated) practices such as linguistic communication and other forms of symbolic interaction. Dialogic cognitive representations thus include and go beyond theoretical constructs such as "identification with others" (Hobson, 1993; Tomasello, 1999), the "like me" stance (Meltzoff & Gopnik, 1993), and "self-other equivalence" (Barresi & Moore, 1996)—which may be ontogenetic forerunners. That is to say, they capture the fact that children both know that they are in some sense equivalent to others—actors can substitute for one another in acts of imitation and role reversal—but at the same time they are different from others. Dialogic cognitive representations thus have built into them the functional equivalence (although not identity) of different participants in activities, one of whom may be the self, but they have additional aspects (e.g., intentions about the other's intentions) deriving from the motivation to share psychological states with others.

This theoretical framework and the current empirical findings raise three important further questions about human development. The first, as alluded to above, is the potential relation between collaborative activities and children's understanding of the decision-making (or rational) dimensions of action and perception. What we have at the moment is a correlation: soon after their first birthdays human infants collaborate and understand an actor's decision-making and rational choices, whereas chimpanzees do neither of these things (again assuming that our results with three young chimpanzees are generalizable to all apes). An interesting theoretical connection between collaboration and the understanding of rational choice is the fact that a key cognitive substrate required for skillful collaboration is the ability to read sub-goals and intentions. That is, in order to collaborate effectively you and I must mesh our action plans at least some of the way down the hierarchy: you will hold the tower steady while I place a block on top—and perhaps we both have to do still other things to prepare for those roles (Bratman, 1992). In many cases all this requires some communication about those plans and sub-plans ahead of time. And so perhaps the need to coordinate plans in collaborative interactions somehow leads to the need to, and the skills for, understanding intentional action at deeper levels.

One can imagine, of course, both a phylogenetic and an ontogenetic story behind this logical relationship. On one hand, one can imagine that there arose at some point in human evolution ecological pressures for collaborative activities involving shared intentionality. Because intention-reading is a critical skill in these—required for meshing sub-plans—those individuals who were best at that would be the ones who were also the best at collaborating and so would be selected. (And of course the same would be true for those individuals who were most motivated to collaborate.) Then in the ontogenetic pathway these skills of intention-reading would just arise, perhaps dependent on all kinds of experience, but not dependent on actual

117

collaborative interactions with others. That is to say, an infant who was deprived of opportunities to collaborate might nevertheless be good at reading intentions and understanding rational choices—even though these were selected for phylogentically to make better collaborators.

The alternative is that the ontogenetic pathway is such that the kinds of triadic collaborative activities in which virtually all children participate, beginning prototypically late in the first year of life, are a necessary prerequisite for children to develop the kinds of intention-reading skills that enable the understanding of decision-making and rational choice—they would set the problem space within which infants would need to read intentions at an especially deep level. In this case, a child who did not participate in collaborative activities would not develop these social-cognitive skills. Perhaps, although not necessarily, infants who live in cultures in which their participation in collaborative activities is encouraged at an early age would develop intention-reading skills earlier. In any case, this is clearly an empirical question that could be answered by either correlational or training studies.

The second question is the origin of dialogic cognitive representations. Again we can imagine both phylogenetic and ontogenetic stories. Perhaps these kinds of cognitive representations were part and parcel of the adaptation enabling human beings to collaborate with one another in the special ways we have described here, and currently in human ontogeny this representational format is simply available for children at some early point in development. On the other hand, it is also possible that what was selected was only the prerequisite social-cognitive and motivational skills for collaboration—most importantly intention-reading and the motivation to share psychological states with others—and dialogic cognitive representations are an ontogenetic product resulting from the internalization of infants various kinds of sharing activities with adults. Following Tomasello et al. (1993) we would assume in this scenario that internalization is a basic (meta-)cognitive process common to at least all primates, but most primates only have individual activities (or very simple social interactions) to internalize whereas humans have special kinds of social/cultural sharing interactions to internalize.

We do not have answers to either of these two questions at this point. Much more data are needed, of all kinds, perhaps most especially: (1) cross-cultural data on the relation between collaboration and intention-reading, (2) correlational and training studies relating these two skills to one another, and (3) correlational and training studies attempting to relate participation in collaborative activities with dialogic cognitive representations—perhaps measured by infants' ability to generalize to novel collaborative contexts.

The third question is exactly what is the sharing line of development and how does it contribute to this overall process? It is possible that certain kinds of social interactions during early ontogeny are necessary ingredients in the emergence of the sharing line of development, but it seems more likely that it is an extremely highly canalized developmental pathway not overly dependent on specific interactions. Babies all over the world begin smiling socially like clockwork at around 6 weeks of age, and they are sharing emotions with others in protoconversations very early as well (Keller, Schölmerich, & Eibl-Eibesfeldt, 1988).

In this case, then, what we need most urgently is a detailed comparison between humans and chimpanzees on the early ontogeny of dyadic social/emotional behaviors. Recent research has shown that chimpanzee infants not only engage in neonatal imitation (Myowa-Yamakoshi et al., 2004), but they also "smile" and engage in en face mutual gazing more than previously thought (Tomonaga, 2003). But their smiles are different from human smiles in function, it would seem, and their mutual gazing seems to occur much less frequently, based on informal observations. Human babies also "coo" when happy, which chimpanzee babies seemingly do not. But most of these conclusions are based on relatively informal observations; more systematic comparisons are needed. Practical difficulties aside, a systematic investigation and comparison of these kinds of phenomena between the two species would help to answer many of our questions about the sharing line of human social-cognitive development.

SOME SPECULATIONS ABOUT HUMAN COGNITIVE PHYLOGENY

Any comparison between apes and humans immediately arouses our curiosity about the evolutionary story involved. Such stories are always woefully underdetermined by the data, but we will nevertheless speculate briefly based on the just-reported data and other recent findings from our and other laboratories. The major theme here is that primates, like all animals, must be competitive in order to survive and procreate, but on top of this competitive nature human beings have developed in addition some special skills and motivations for interacting with one another collaboratively.

There is no question that on the whole primates are intensely competitive creatures. And by most accounts, the social-cognitive skills that distinguish primates from other mammals evolved mainly in the context of competitive social interactions. Following Humphrey (1976), primate social cognition has often been characterized by appellations such as primate politics (de Waal, 1982) and Machiavellian intelligence (Byrne & Whiten, 1988). And indeed, in experimental comparisons, chimpanzees seem to show their most sophisticated social-cognitive skills in competitive rather than in cooperative situations. Two examples will suffice.

First, after many years of negative findings on the question of whether chimpanzees understand what others see and know—both from our own laboratory and those of others—we noticed that all of the existing tests essentially asked chimpanzees to determine what another person did or did not see (or know) in a cooperative/communicative paradigm; for example, following the pointing gesture of a knowledgeable versus an ignorant human in a food finding situation (Povinelli, Rulf, & Bierschwale, 1994; Call & Tomasello, 1999). But then we devised a competitive paradigm where the chimpanzee's task was to compete with another chimpanzee over food in a situation in which its competitor either could or could not see some food (Hare, Call, Agnetta, & Tomasello, 2000; Hare, Call, & Tomasello, 2001). In this paradigm, the chimpanzees looked completely different, with subordinates skillfully going for the food that only they could see.

Second, as noted above, chimpanzees and other primates typically perform very poorly in the Understanding Communicative Intentions task as administered in the current study. Hare and Tomasello (2004) therefore devised a competitive version of the task. In this version, a human first interacted with the chimpanzee competitively by "stealing" food that the chimpanzee might potentially have gotten for itself through a hole in the Plexiglas. Then, instead of pointing to the bucket with food—as in the classic task—this same competitor reached futilely for one of the buckets for himself (he was constrained by the physical situation) without attempting to communicate with the chimpanzee at all (e.g., never looking at the chimpanzee). In doing this, the human's extended arm was very similar physically to a pointing gesture. In this situation, all of a sudden chimpanzees knew where the food was (and the same individuals failed, as usual, when a cooperative human in the same study pointed to the location of the hidden food). So one might say that chimpanzees do not understand a human's communicative intention to help them locate the hidden food cooperatively, but they do understand a human's simple intention to obtain the food for himself competitively, making relevant inferences from that goal-directed behavior.

Our proposal is that in addition to competing with others (and coordinating with others generally, like all social animals), human beings also evolved skills and motivations for collaborating with one another in activities involving shared intentionality. At some point—perhaps heralding the emergence of modern humans some 150,000 years ago—individuals who were able to collaborate together more effectively in various social activities came to have a selective advantage. This may have happened within groups, in a manner analogous to the hypothesis of Wrangham (1980), who argues that because many primates forage for patchy resources such as fruit, and patchy resources may be easily dominated by a small group of individuals to the exclusion of others, some primates have evolved social systems in which small groups act together so as to compete with groupmates for valued resources (see also Van Schaik, 1989). Humans may simply have pushed this process—small bands acting together to compete with other bands in their group—a bit further by turning "acting together" into collaborating. But the evolution of humans' unique skills of collaboration may also have happened between groups. Thus, it is also possible that some kind of group-level selection (cultural group selection) played an important role in the evolution of these collaborative activities, as some change in the ecology of *Homo* made it more likely that entire groups with many collaborators outcompeted other groups with fewer collaborators (Sober & Wilson, 1998; Richerson & Boyd, 2004). This led to all kinds of collaborative, symbolic, and institutional structures, including those in which important information is stored externally by human beings in such things as books and pictures (Donald, 1991).

Another important component to the story might be human communication. As noted in many places above, the human version of communication is much more collaborative than that of any other primate species: the structure of conversation is collaborative, the structure of symbols is collaborative, the motive is often cooperative, and the expression of communicative intentions in deictic gestures or symbols requires a joint attentional format as common communicative background to make sense. In this context, the evolutionary speculation of Dunbar (1996) is especially interesting, as he posits that linguistic communication did not evolve for helping humans to coordinate their instrumental activities, but rather it evolved for simply gossiping—as a kind of social glue (analogous to primate grooming), so that humans could share information with one another freely in a cooperative, not competitive spirit (which would of course have many benefits). In this scenario, simply sharing experience communicatively would be the original collaborative act.

Finally, one especially interesting story that fits well with our emphasis on humans as special cooperators is that of Wrangham (in press). He notes that domesticated animal species are typically more gracile, than their undomesticated progenitors. Interestingly, the main characteristic that distinguishes the skeletons of modern humans from those of their immediate ancestors is gracility. So perhaps modern humans somehow domesticated themselves, mainly by excluding from the group those who were too aggressive or did not cooperate appropriately—and indeed one could argue that moral norms have arisen precisely to do something like this. Wrangham also notes, following Boehm (1999), that human hunter-gatherers typically never let one individual get too aggressive or too powerful; when that happens, the rest of them gang up on that individual and either kill him or exile him. Wrangham also hypothesizes that the use of a system of communication that could deal with events displaced in space and time would be

121

critical for planning such subterfuge. Speculative although it may be, this story is interesting in the current perspective because it essentially says that a key way that humans became more cooperative was by cooperating to get rid of the noncooperators. It would be nice if this story were true.

CONCLUSIONS

In our view, what makes human cognition so different from that of other animal species is, in a word, culture. An individual human's ability to navigate in the forest is nothing special comparatively, but with maps and a GPS it becomes so. An untrained (and nonlinguistic) human's quantitative skills are probably not so special comparatively, but with training in the use of Arabic numerals and computational procedures they become so. Following Vygotsky (1978), Tomasello (1999) emphasized that uniquely human cognition mainly arose from the fact that cultures create cognitively complex material and symbolic artifacts over historical time, and these mediate developing children's cognitive interactions with their environment. To acquire the appropriate use of these mediating artifacts, children need to be able to engage in various kinds of cultural learning, which depend on the social-cognitive skills for reading intentions. Supplementing this focus on cultural learning is our current emphasis on cultural creation in which human children participate in the creation of collaborative social interactions with others. Cultural learning and creation are both part of the same overall process, of course, but our revised view—forced upon us, as it were, by the empirical fact that chimpanzees do seem to understand important aspects of intentional action and perception—is that it is collaborative skills and motivations involving shared intentionality that are most clearly and uniquely human.

In any case, whatever the "true" story turns out to be, it seems undeniable that humans differentiate themselves from other primates in the amount and degree to which they collaborate with one another to achieve common goals, share experiences communicatively just for the sake of sharing, help one another "altruistically," build cultural practices and institutions, and in general depend on one another and their forebears for virtually all of the important things in their lives. To explain this fact one needs to tell a set of interconnected stories in phylogenetic, cultural-historical, and ontogenetic time.

REFERENCES

Antinucci, F. (1989). *Cognitive structure and development in nonhuman primates*. Hillsdale, NJ: Lawrence Erlbaum Associates.

Bakeman, R., & Adamson, L. (1984). Coordinating attention to people and objects in mother–infant and peer–infant interactions. *Child Development*, **55**, 1278–1289.

Baldwin, D. A., Baird, J. A., Saylor, M. M., & Clark, M. A. (2001). Infants parse dynamic action. *Child Development*, **72**, 708–717.

Bard, K. A., Platzman, K. A., Lester, B. M., & Suomi, S. J. (1992). Orientation to social and nonsocial stimuli in neonatal chimpanzees and humans. *Infant Behavior and Development*, **15**, 43–56.

Bard, K. A., & Vauclair, J. (1984). The communicative context of object manipulation in ape and human adult–infant pairs. *Journal of Human Evolution*, **13** (2), 181–190.

Baron-Cohen, S. (1995). *Mindblindness: An essay on autism and theory of mind*. Cambridge, MA: MIT Press.

Barresi, J., & Moore, C. (1996). Intentional relations and social understanding. *Behavioral and Brain Sciences*, **19** (1), 107–129.

Bates, E. (1979). *The emergence of symbols: Cognition and communication in infancy*. New York: Academic Press.

Beach, F. (1950). The snark was a boojum. *American Psychologist*, **5**, 115–124.

Behne, T., Carpenter, M., Call, J., & Tomasello, M. (2005). Unwilling versus unable? Infants' understanding of intentional action. *Developmental Psychology*, **41**, 328–337.

Behne, T., Carpenter, M., & Tomasello, M. (in press). One-year-olds comprehend the communicative intentions behind gestures in a hiding game. *Developmental Science*.

Bellagamba, F., & Tomasello, M. (1999). Re-enacting intended acts: Comparing 12- and 18-month-olds. *Infant Behavior & Development*, **22**, 277–282.

Bering, J. M., Bjorklund, D. F., & Ragan, P. (2000). Deferred imitation of object-related actions in human-reared juvenile chimpanzees and orangutans. *Developmental Psychobiology*, **36**, 218–232.

Bertenthal, B. (1996). Origins and early development of perception, action, and representation. *Annual Review of Psychology*, **47**, 431–459.

Bitterman, M. (1965). Phyletic differences in learning. *American Psychologist*, **20**, 396–410.

Bjorklund, D. F., Bering, J. M., & Ragan, P. (2000). A two-year longitudinal study of deferred imitation of object manipulation in a juvenile chimpanzee (*Pan troglodytes*) and orangutan (*Pan pygmaeus*). *Developmental Psychobiology*, **37**, 229–237.

Boehm, C. (1999). *Hierarchy in the forest: The evolution of egalitarian behavior*. Cambridge, MA: Harvard University Press.

Boesch, C., & Boesch, H. (1989). Hunting behavior of wild chimpanzees in the Tai-National-Park. *American Journal of Physical Anthropology*, **78** (4), 547–573.

Braten, S. (Ed.) (2000). *Modellmakt og altersentriske spedbarn*. Bergen: Sigma.

Bratman, M. E. (1992). Shared cooperative activity. *Philosophical Review*, **101** (2), 327–341.

Bräuer, J., Call, J., & Tomasello, M. (in press). All four great ape species follow gaze around barriers. *Journal of Comparative Psychology*.

Brooks, R., & Meltzoff, A. N. (2002). The importance of eyes: How infants interpret adult looking behavior. *Developmental Psychology*, **38**, 958–966.

Brownell, C. A., & Carriger, M. S. (1990). Changes in cooperation and self-other differentiation during the second year. *Child Development*, **61**, 1164–1174.

Butler, S. C., Caron, A. J., & Brooks, R. (2000). Infant understanding of the referential nature of looking. *Journal of Cognition and Development*, **4**, 359–377.

Butterworth, G., & Cochran, E. (1980). Towards a mechanism of joint visual attention in human infancy. *International Journal of Behavioral Development*, **19**, 253–272.

Butterworth, G., & Jarrett, N. (1991). What minds have in common is space: Spatial mechanisms serving joint visual attention in infancy. *British Journal of Developmental Psychology*, **9**, 55–72.

Byrne, R. W., & Whiten, A. (1988). *Machiavellian intelligence. Social expertise and the evolution of intellect in monkeys, apes, and humans*. New York: Oxford University Press.

Call, J. (2001). Chimpanzee social cognition. *Trends in Cognitive Sciences*, **5**, 369–405.

Call, J., Agnetta, B., & Tomasello, M. (2000). Social cues that chimpanzees do and do not use to locate hidden objects. *Animal Cognition*, **3**, 23–34.

Call, J., & Carpenter, M. (2003). On imitation in apes and children. *Infancia y aprendizaje*, **26**, 325–349.

Call, J., Carpenter, M., & Tomasello, M. (in press). Focusing on outcomes and focusing on actions in the process of social learning: Chimpanzees and human children. *Animal Cognition*.

Call, J., Hare, B., Carpenter, M., & Tomasello, M. (2004). Unwilling or unable: Chimpanzees' understanding of human intentional action. *Developmental Science*, **7**, 488–498.

Call, J., Hare, B., & Tomasello, M. (1998). Chimpanzee gaze following in an object choice task. *Animal Cognition*, **1**, 89–100.

Call, J., & Tomasello, M. (1994). The social learning of tool use by orangutans (*Pongo pygmaeus*). *Human Evolution*, **9**, 297–313.

Call, J., & Tomasello, M. (1995). The use of social information in the problem-solving of orangutans (*Pongo pygmaeus*) and human children (*Homo sapiens*). *Journal of Comparative Psychology*, **109**, 308–320.

Call, J., & Tomasello, M. (1996). The effect of humans in the cognitive development of apes. In A. Russon, K. Bard, & S. Parker (Eds.), *Reaching into thought: The minds of the great apes* (pp. 371–403). Cambridge, MA: Cambridge University Press.

Call, J., & Tomasello, M. (1998). Distinguishing intentional from accidental actions in orangutans (*Pongo pygmaeus*), chimpanzees (*Pan troglodytes*) and human children (*Homo sapiens*). *Journal of Comparative Psychology*, **112**, 192–206.

Call, J., & Tomasello, M. (1999). A nonverbal false belief task: The performance of children and great apes. *Child Development*, **70**, 381–395.

Call, J., & Tomasello, M. (in press). What do chimpanzees know about seeing revisited: An explanation of the third kind. In N. Eilan, C. Hoerl, T. McCormack, & J. Roessler (Eds.), *Issues in joint attention*. Oxford: Oxford University Press.

Camaioni, L. (1993). The development of intentional communication: A re-analysis. In J. Nadel & L. Camaioni (Eds.), *New perspectives in early communicative development* (pp. 82–96). New York: Routledge.

Caron, A. J., Butler, S. C., & Brooks, R. (2002). Gaze following at 12 and 14 months: Do the eyes matter? *British Journal of Developmental Psychology*, **20**, 225–239.

Carpendale, J. I. M., & Lewis, C. (2004). Constructing an understanding of mind: The development of children's social understanding within social interaction. *Behavioral and Brain Sciences*, **24**, 79–96.

Carpenter, M., Akhtar, N., & Tomasello, M. (1998). Fourteen- through 18-month-old infants differentially imitate intentional and accidental actions. *Infant Behavior & Development*, **21**, 315–330.

Carpenter, M., & Call, J. (in press). The question of 'what to imitate': Inferring goals and intentions from demonstrations. In K. Dautenhahn & C. Nehaniv (Eds.), *Imitation and social learning in robots, humans and animals: Behavioural, social and communicative dimensions*. Cambridge: Cambridge University Press.

Carpenter, M., Call, J., & Tomasello, M. (2002). Understanding 'prior intentions' enables 2-year-olds to imitatively learn a complex task. *Child Development*, **73**, 1431–1441.

Carpenter, M., Call, J., & Tomasello, M. (2005). Twelve- and 18-month-olds imitate actions in terms of goals. *Developmental Science*, **8**, 18–20.

Carpenter, M., Nagell, K., & Tomasello, M. (1998). Social cognition, joint attention, and communicative competencies from 9 to 15 months of age. *Monographs of the Society of Research in Child Development*, **63** (4).

Carpenter, M., Pennington, B. F., & Rogers, S. J. (2002). Interrelations among social-cognitive skills in young children with autism and developmental delays. *Journal of Autism and Developmental Disorders*, **32**, 91–106.

Carpenter, M., Tomasello, M., & Savage-Rumbaugh, S. (1995). Joint attention and imitative learning in children, chimpanzees, and enculturated chimpanzees. *Social Development*, **4**, 18–37.

Carpenter, M., Tomasello, M., & Striano, T. (in press). Role reversal imitation and language in typically-developing infants and children with autism. *Infancy*.

Carver, C. S., & Scheier, M. F. (1982). Control theory: A useful conceptual framework for personality—social, clinical, and health psychology. *Psychological Bulletin*, **92**, 111–135.

Chalmeau, R. (1994). Do chimpanzees cooperate in a learning task? *Primates*, **35** (3), 385–392.

Cheney, D. L., & Seyfarth, R. M. (1990). *How monkeys see the world: Inside the mind of another species*. Chicago: The University of Chicago Press.

Chevalier-Skolnikoff, S. (1977). A Piagetian model for comparing the socialization of monkey, ape, and human infants. In S. Chevalier-Skolnikoff & F. Poirier (Eds.), *Primate biosocial development* (pp. 159–188). New York: Garland.

Chevalier-Skolnikoff, S. (1989). Spontaneous tool use and sensorimotor intelligence in Cebus compared with other monkeys and apes. *Behavioral and Brain Sciences*, **12**, 561–627.

Clark, E. V. (1997). Conceptual perspective and lexical choice in acquisition. *Cognition*, **64** (1), 1–37.

Clark, H. (1996). *Uses of language*. Cambridge: Cambridge University Press.

Corkum, V., & Moore, C. (1995). Development of joint visual attention in infants. In C. Moore & P. J. Dunham (Eds.), *Joint attention: Its origins and role in development*. Hillsdale, NJ: Erlbaum.

Crawford, M. P. (1937). The cooperative solving of problems by young chimpanzees. *Comparative Psychology Monographs*, **14**, 1–88.

Csibra, G. (2003). Teleological and referential understanding of action in infancy. *Philosophical Transactions of the Royal Society, London B*, **358**, 447–458.

Csibra, G., Biró, S., Koós, O., & Gergely, G. (2002). One year old infants use teleological representation of actions productively. *Cognitive Science*, **104**, 1–23.

Csibra, G., Gergely, G., Bíró, S., Koós, O., & Brockbank, M. (1999). Goal attribution without agency cues: The perception of 'pure reason' in infancy. *Cognition*, **72**, 237–267.

Custance, D. M., Whiten, A., & Bard, K. (1995). Can young chimpanzees imitate arbitrary actions? Hayes and Hayes (1952) revisited. *Behaviour*, **132**, 839–858.

D'Entremont, B., Hains, S. M. J., & Muir, D. W. (1997). A demonstration of gaze following in 3- to 6-month-olds. *Infant Behavior & Development*, **20** (4), 569–572.

de Waal, F. B. M. (1982). *Chimpanzee politics*. London: Jonathan Cape.

Dunbar, R. (1996). *Grooming, gossip and the evolution of language*. London: Faber Faber and Harvard University Press.

Eckerman, C. O. (1996). Early social-communicative development: Illustrative developmental analyses. In R. B. Cairns et al. (Eds.), *Developmental science*. New York: Cambridge University Press.

Eibl-Eibesfeldt, I. (1970). *Ethology: The biology of behavior*. New York: Holt, Rinehart, Winston.

Fernyhough, C. (1996). The dialogic mind: A dialogic approach to the higher mental functions. *New Ideas in Psychology*, **14**, 47–62.

Flavell, J. (1977). *Cognitive development*. Englewood Cliffs, NJ: Prentice-Hall.

Flom, R., Deák, G. O., Phill, C., & Pick, A. D. (2003). Nine-month-olds' shared visual attention as a function of gesture and object location. *Infant Behavior and Development*, **27**, 181–194.

Franco, F., & Butterworth, G. (1996). Pointing and social awareness: Declaring and requesting in the second year. *Journal of Child Language*, **23**, 307–336.

Garcia, J., & Koelling, R. (1966). The relation of cue to consequent in avoidance learning. *Psychonomic Science*, **4**, 123–124.

Gardner, R. A., Gardner, B. T., & van Cantfort, T. E. (Eds.) (1989). *Teaching sign language to chimpanzees*. Albany: SUNY Press.

Gergely, G. (2001). The obscure object of desire: 'Nearly, but clearly not, like me': Contingency preference in normal children versus children with autism. In K. J. Zerbe (Ed.), *Bulletin of the Menninger Clinic* (pp. 411–426). New York: Guilford.

Gergely, G., Bekkering, H., & Király, I. (2002). Rational imitation in preverbal infants. *Nature*, **415**, 755.

Gergely, G., & Csibra, G. (2003). Teleological reasoning in infancy: The naive theory of rational action. *Trends in Cognitive Sciences*, **7**, 287–292.

Gergely, G., Nádasdy, Z., Csibra, G., & Bíró, S. (1995). Taking the intentional stance at 12 months of age. *Cognition*, **56**, 165–193.

Gergeley, G., & Watson, J. (1999). Early socio-emotional development: Contingency perception and the social-biofeedback model. In P. Rochat (Ed.), *Early social cognition*. Mahwah, NJ: Erlbaum.

Gibson, E., & Rader, N. (1979). Attention: The perceiver as performer. In G. Hale & M. Lewis (Eds.), *Attention and cognitive development* (pp. 6–36). New York: Plenum Press.

Gibson, J. J. (1966). *The senses considered as a perceptual system*. Boston: Houghton-Mifflin.

Gibson, K. R. (1986). Cognition, brain size and the extraction of embedded food resources. In J. G. Else & P. C. Lee (Eds.), *Primate ontogeny, cognition and social behaviour* (pp. 93–103). Cambridge: Cambridge University Press.

Gilbert, M. (1989). *On social facts. International Library of Philosophy*. London: Routledge; Princeton, NJ: Princeton University Press.

Golinkoff, R. (1993). When is communication a meeting of the minds? *Journal of Child Language*, **20**, 199–208.

Gómez, J.-C. (1996). Nonhuman primate theories of (nonhuman primate) minds: Some issues concerning the origins of mindreading. In P. Carruthers & P. K. Smith (Eds.), *Theories of theories of mind* (pp. 330–343). Cambridge: Cambridge University Press.

Goodall, J. (1986). *Chimpanzees of the Gombe*. Cambridge, MA: Harvard University Press.

Greenfield, P. M., & Savage-Rumbaugh, E. S. (1991). Imitation, grammatical development, and the invention of protogrammar by an ape. In N. A. Krasnegor, D. M. Rumbaugh, R. L. Schiefelbusch, & M. Studdert-Kennedy (Eds.), *Biological and behavioral determinants of language development* (pp. 235–258). Hillsdale, NJ: Lawrence Earlbaum Associates.

Hare, B., Call, J., Agnetta, B., & Tomasello, M. (2000). Chimpanzees know what conspecifics do and do not see. *Animal Behaviour*, **59**, 771–785.

Hare, B., Call, J., & Tomasello, M. (2001). Do chimpanzees know what conspecifics know? *Animal Behaviour*, **61** (1), 139–151.

Hare, B., Call, J., & Tomasello, M. (in press). Chimpanzees deceive a human by hiding. *Cognition*.

Hare, B., & Tomasello, M. (2004). Chimpanzees are more skillful in competitive than in cooperative cognitive tasks. *Animal Behaviour*, **68**, 571–581.

Hay, D. F. (1979). Cooperative interactions and sharing between very young children and their parents. *Developmental Psychology*, **15**, 647–653.

Hay, D. F., & Murray, P. (1982). Giving and requesting: Social facilitation of infants' offers to adults. *Infant Behavior and Development*, **5**, 301–310.

Hayes, C. (1952). *Ape in our house*. New York: Harper.

Hayes, K. J., & Hayes, C. (1952). Imitation in a home-raised chimpanzee. *Journal of Comparative and Physiological Psychology*, **45**, 450–459.

Hobson, R. P. (1993). *Autism and the development of mind*. Mahwah, NJ: Erlbaum.

Hobson, R. P. (2002). *The cradle of thought*. London: Macmillan.

Hobson, R. P., & Lee, A. (1999). Imitation and identification in autism. *Journal of Child Psychology & Psychiatry*, **40**, 649–659.

Hodos, W., & Campbell, C. B. G. (1969). Scala naturae: Why there is no theory in comparative psychology. *Psychological Review*, **76**, 337–350.

Huang, C.-T., Heyes, C. M., & Charman, T. (2002). Infants' behavioral re-enactment of 'failed attempts': Exploring the roles of emulation learning, stimulus enhancement and understanding of intentions. *Developmental Psychology*, **38**, 840–855.

Humphrey, N. K. (1976). The social function of intellect. In P. Bateson & R. Hine (Eds.), *Growing points in ethology*. Cambridge: Cambridge University Press.

Itakura, S. (1996). An exploratory study of gaze-monitoring in nonhuman primates. *Japanese Psychological Research*, **38**, 174–180.

Johnson, S. C., Booth, A., & O'Hearn, K. (2001). Inferring the goals of a nonhuman agent. *Cognitive Development*, **16**, 637–656.

Kaminski, J., Call, J., & Tomasello, M. (2004). Body orientation and face orientation: Two factors controlling apes' begging behavior from humans. *Animal Cognition*, **7**, 216–223.

Kaye, K. (1982). *The mental and social life of babies: How parents create persons*. Chicago: University of Chicago Press.

Keller, H., Schö lmerich, A., & Eibl-Eibesfeldt, I. (1988). Communication patterns in adult-infant interactions in western and non-western cultures. *Journal of Cross-Cultural Psychology*, **19**, 427–445.

Kellogg, W., & Kellogg, L. (1933). *Development of ape and child*. New York: McGraw Hill.

Király, I. (2002). *Az emlékezet fejlődése kisgyermekkorban: Utánzás és emlékezet [The development of memory in young children: Imitation and memory]*. Budapest: Gondolat.

Ladygina-Kohts, N. N. (2002). *Infant chimpanzee and human child: A classic 1935 comparative study of ape emotions and intelligence*. New York: Oxford University Press.

Lehmann, H., Call, J., & Tomasello, M. (in preparation). Gaze following in infants and chimpanzees.

Leslie, A. (1984). Infant perception of a manual pick up event. *British Journal of Developmental Psychology*, **2**, 19–32.

Liszkowski, U., Carpenter, M., Henning, A., Striano, T., & Tomasello, M. (2004). 12-month-olds point to share attention and interest. *Developmental Science*, **7**, 297–307.

Liszkowski, U., Carpenter, M., Striano, T., & Tomasello, M. (in press). Twelve- and 18-month-olds point to provide information for others.

Maestripieri, D., & Call, J. (1994). Mother–infant communication in primates. In C. T. Snowdon (Ed.), *Advances in the study of behavior* (**Vol. 24**). New York: Academic Press.

Meltzoff, A. (1995). Understanding the intentions of others: Re-enactment of intended acts by 18-month-old children. *Developmental Psychology*, **31**, 1–16.

Meltzoff, A. N., & Gopnik, A. (1993). The role of imitation in understanding persons and developing a theory of mind. In S. Baron-Cohen, H. Tager-Flusberg, & D. J. Cohen (Eds.), *Understanding other minds: Perspectives from autism* (pp. 335–366). New York: Oxford.

Merlin, D. (1991). *Origins of the modern mind*. Cambridge: Harvard University Press.

Michotte, A. (1963). *The perception of causality*. London: Methuen.

Mizuno, Y., & Takashita, H. (2002). Behavioral development of chimpanzees in the first month of life: Observation of mother–infant pairs at night. *Japanese Psychological Review*, **45**, 352–364.

Moll, H., Koring, C., Carpenter, M., & Tomasello, M. (submitted). Infants determine what others attend to by pragmatics and exclusion.

Moll, H., & Tomasello, M. (2004). 12- and 18-month-olds follow gaze to hidden locations. *Developmental Science*, **7**, F1–F9.

Moore, C. (1996). Theories of mind in infancy. *British Journal of Developmental Psychology*, **14**, 19–40.

Moore, C., & Corkum, V. L. (1998). Infant gaze following based on eye direction. *British Journal of Developmental Psychology*, **16**, 495–503.

Mundy, P., Sigman, M., Ungerer, J., & Sherman, T. (1987). Nonverbal communication and play correlates of language development in autistic children. *Journal of Autism and Developmental Disorders*, **17**, 349–364.

Myowa, M. (1996). Imitation of facial gestures by an infant chimpanzee. *Primates*, **37**, 207–213.

Myowa-Yamakoshi, M., & Matsuzawa, T. (2000). Imitation of intentional manipulatory actions in chimpanzees. *Journal of Comparative Psychology*, **114**, 381–391.

Myowa-Yamakoshi, M., Tomonaga, M., Tanaka, M., & Matsuzawa, T. (2004). Imitation in neonatal chimpanzees (*Pan troglodytes*). *Developmental Science*, **7** (4), 437–442.

Nagell, K., Olguin, K., & Tomasello, M. (1993). Processes of social learning in the tool use of chimpanzees (*Pan troglodytes*) and human children (*Homo sapiens*). *Journal of Comparative Psychology*, **107**, 174–186.

Okamoto, S., Tomonaga, M., Ishii, K., Kawai, N., Tanaka, M., & Matsuzawa, T. (2002). An infant chimpanzee (*Pan troglodytes*) follows human gaze. *Animal Cognition*, **5**, 107–114.

Owren, M. J., & Rendall, D. (2001). Sound on the rebound: Returning form and function to the forefront in understanding nonhuman primate vocal signaling. *Evolutionary Anthropology*, **10** (2), 58–71.

Parker, S., & McKinney, M. (1999). *Origins of intelligence: The evolution of cognitive development in monkeys, apes, and humans*. Baltimore: Johns Hopkins Press.

Perner, J. (1991). *Understanding the representational mind*. Cambridge, MA: MIT Press.

Perucchini, P., & Camaioni, L. (1993). *When intentional communication emerges? Developmental dissociations between declarative and imperative functions of the pointing gesture*. Paper presented at the Developmental Conference of the British Psychological Society, Birmingham.

Phillips, W., Baron-Cohen, S., & Rutter, M. (1992). The role of eye contact in goal detection: Evidence from normal infants and children with autism or mental handicap. *Development and Psychopathology*, **4**, 375–383.

Plooij, F. X. (1984). *The behavioral development of free-living chimpanzee babies and infants*. Norwood, NJ: Ablex.

Povinelli, D. (1991). *Social intelligence in monkeys and apes.* Unpublished doctoral dissertation, Yale University, New Haven, CT.

Povinelli, D., & Eddy, T. J. (1996). What young chimpanzees know about seeing. *Monographs of the Society for Research in Child Development*, **61** (3).

Povinelli, D., Nelson, K. E., & Boysen, S. T. (1990). Inferences about guessing and knowing by chimpanzees (*Pan troglodytes*). *Journal of Comparative Psychology*, **104**, 203–210.

Povinelli, D., Nelson, K. E., & Boysen, S. T. (1992). Comprehension of role reversal in chimpanzees: Evidence of empathy? *Animal Behaviour*, **43**, 633–640.

Povinelli, D., Perilloux, H., Reaux, J., & Bierschwale, D. (1998). Young chimpanzees' reactions to intentional versus accidental and inadvertent actions. *Behavioural Processes*, **42**, 205–218.

Povinelli, D., Rulf, A. B., & Bierschwale, D. T. (1994). Absence of knowledge attribution and self-recognition in young chimpanzees (*Pan troglodytes*). *Journal of Comparative Psychology*, **108**, 74–80.

Povinelli, D. J., & O'Neill, D. (2000). Do chimpanzees use their gestures to instruct each other? In S. Baron-Cohen, H. Tager-Flusberg, & D. Cohen (Eds.), *Understanding other minds: Perspectives from developmental cognitive neuroscience* (2nd ed.). Oxford: Oxford University Press.

Povinelli, D. J., & Vonk, J. (2003). Chimpanzee minds: Suspiciously human? *Trends in Cognitive Sciences*, **7** (4), 157–160.

Premack, D., & Woodruff, G. (1978). Does the chimpanzee have a theory of mind? *Behavioral and Brain Sciences*, **4**, 515–526.

Ratner, N., & Bruner, J. (1978). Games, social exchange and the acquisition of language. *Journal of Child Language*, **5**, 391–401.

Reaux, J. E., Theall, L. A., & Povinelli, D. J. (1999). A longitudinal investigation of chimpanzees' understanding of visual perception. *Child Development*, **70**, 275–290.

Richerson, P., & Boyd, R. (2004). *Not by genes alone.* Chicago: University of Chicago Press.

Rochat, P., & Striano, T. (1999). Social-cognitive development in the first year. In P. Rochat (Ed.), *Early social cognition.* Mahwah, NJ: Erlbaum.

Rosenthal, R. (1991). *Meta-analytic procedures for social research.* London: Sage.

Ross, H. S., & Lollis, S. P. (1987). Communication within infant social games. *Developmental Psychology*, **23** (2), 241–248.

Russon, A., & Galdikas, B. (1993). Imitation in free-ranging rehabilitant orangutans (*Pongo pygmaeus*). *Journal of Comparative Psychology*, **107** (2), 147–161.

Santos, L. R., & Hauser, M. D. (1999). How monkeys see the eyes: Cotton-top tamarins' reaction to changes in visual attention and action. *Animal Cognition*, **2** (3), 131–139.

Saussure, F. (1916/1959). *Course in general linguistics.* New York: Philosophical Library.

Savage-Rumbaugh, S. (1990). Language as a cause–effect communication system. *Philosophical Psychology*, **3**, 55–76.

Savage-Rumbaugh, S., & Lewin, R. (1994). *Kanzi: The ape at the brink of the human mind.* New York: Wiley.

Savage-Rumbaugh, E. S., Rumbaugh, D. M., & Boysen, S. (1978). Linguistically mediated tool use and exchange by chimpanzees (*Pan troglodytes*). *Behavioral and Brain Sciences*, **4**, 539–554.

Savage-Rumbaugh, E. S., Shanker, S., & Tolbert, T. (1998). *Apes, language and the human mind.* New York: Oxford University Press.

Scheffelin, B., & Ochs, E. (1986). *Language socialization across cultures.* Cambridge: Cambridge University Press.

Searle, J. (1995). *The construction of social reality.* New York: Free Press.

Sober, E., & Wilson, D. S. (1998). *Unto others: The evolution and psychology of unselfish behavior.* Cambridge, MA: Harvard University Press.

Sommerville, J. A., & Woodward, A. L. (2005). Pulling out the intentional structure of action: The relation between action processing and action production in infancy. *Cognition*, **95**, 1–30.

Sperber, D., & Wilson, D. (1986). *Relevance: Communication and cognition.* Cambridge, MA: Harvard University Press.

Stern, D. N. (1985). *The interpersonal world of the infant.* New York: Basic Books.

Tomasello, M. (1995). Joint attention as social cognition. In C. Moore & P. J. Dunham (Eds.), *Joint attention. Its origin and role in development* (pp. 103–130). Hillsdale, NJ: Lawrence Erlbaum.

Tomasello, M. (1996). Do apes ape? In C. M. Heyes & B. G. Galef, Jr. (Eds.), *Social learning in animals: The roots of culture.* New York: Academic Press.

Tomasello, M. (1998). Reference: Intending that others jointly attend. *Pragmatics and Cognition*, **6**, 229–244.

Tomasello, M. (1999). *The cultural origins of human cognition.* Cambridge, MA: Harvard University Press.

Tomasello, M., & Call, J. (1997). *Primate cognition.* Oxford: Oxford University Press.

Tomasello, M., & Call, J. (2004). The role of humans in the cognitive development of apes revisited. *Animal Cognition*, **7**, 213–215.

Tomasello, M., Call, J., & Hare, B. (1998). Five primate species follow the visual gaze of conspecifics. *Animal Behaviour*, **55** (4), 1063–1069.

Tomasello, M., Call, J., & Hare, B. (2003). Chimpanzees understand psychological states: The question is which ones and to what extent. *Trends in Cognitive Science*, **7**, 153–156.

Tomasello, M., Call, J., Nagell, K., Olguin, R., & Carpenter, M. (1994). The learning and use of gestural signals by young chimpanzees: A trans-generational study. *Primates*, **37**, 137–154.

Tomasello, M., Call, J., Warren, J., Frost, T., Carpenter, M., & Nagell, K. (1997). The ontogeny of chimpanzee gestural signals: A comparison across groups and generations. *Evolution of Communication*, **1**, 223–253.

Tomasello, M., Carpenter, M., Call, J., Behne, T., & Moll, H. (in press). Understanding and sharing intentions: The origins of cultural cognition. *Behavioral and Brain Sciences*.

Tomasello, M., & Haberl, K. (2003). Understanding attention: 12- and 18-month-olds know what is new for other persons. *Developmental Psychology*, **39** (5), 906–912.

Tomasello, M., Hare, B., & Agnetta, B. (1999). Chimpanzees, *Pan troglodytes*, follow gaze direction geometrically. *Animal Behaviour*, **58** (4), 769–777.

Tomasello, M., Hare, B., & Fogleman, T. (2001). The ontogeny of gaze following in chimpanzees and rhesus macaques. *Animal Behaviour*, **61**, 335–343.

Tomasello, M., Kruger, A., & Ratner, H. (1993). Cultural learning. *Behavioral and Brain Sciences*, **16**, 495–552.

Tomasello, M., Petschauer, H., & Carpenter, M. (in preparation). *Infants copy behavioral "style" in an imitation task.*

Tomasello, M., & Rakoczy, H. (2003). What makes human cognition unique? From individual to shared to collective intentionality. *Mind and Language*, **18** (2), 121–147.

Tomasello, M., Savage-Rumbaugh, S., & Kruger, A. (1993). Imitative learning of actions on objects by children, chimpanzees and enculturated chimpanzees. *Child Development*, **64**, 1688–1705.

Tomonaga, M. (2003). *Infant chimpanzee social cognition.* Presentation to MPI-EVA.

Tomonaga, M., Tanaka, M., Matsuzawa, T., Myowa-Yamakoshi, M., Kosugi, D., Mizuno, Y., Okamoto, S., Yamaguchi, M. K., & Bard, K. A. (2004). Development of social cognition in infant chimpanzees (*Pan troglodytes*): Face recognition, smiling, gaze, and the lack of triadic interactions. *Japanese Psychological Research*, **46**, 227–235.

Trevarthen, C. (1979). Instincts for human understanding and for cultural cooperation: Their development in infancy. In M. von Cranach, K. Foppa, W. Lepenies & D. Ploog (Eds.), *Human ethology: Claims and limits of a new discipline*. Cambridge: Cambridge University Press.

Tuomela, R. (1995). *The importance of us: A philosophical study of basic social notion*. Stanford: Stanford University Press.

Turner, L., Pozdol, S., Ulman, T. C., & Stone, W. (2003). *The relation between social-communicative skills and language development in young children with autism*. Poster presented at the meetings of the Society for Research in Child Development, Tampa, FL.

Uller, C. (2004). Disposition to recognize goals in infant chimpanzees (*Pan troglodytes*). *Animal Cognition*, **7**, 154–161.

Uzgiris, I. C., & Hunt, J. M. V. (1975). *Assessment in infancy: Ordinal scales of psychological development*. Urbana: University of Illinois Press.

van Schaik, C. P. (1989). The ecology of social relationships amongst female primates. In V. Standen & R. Foley (Eds.), *Comparative socioecology: The behavioral ecology of humans and other mammals* (pp. 195–218). Oxford: Blackwell Scientific.

Verba, M. (1994). The beginnings of collaboration in peer interaction. *Human Development*, **37** (3), 125–139.

Vygotsky, L. (1978). *Mind in society: The development of higher psychological processes*. Harvard: Harvard University Press.

Warneken, F., Chen, F., & Tomasello, M. (submitted). *Collaboration in children and chimpanzees*.

Wellman, H. (1990). *The child's theory of mind*. Cambridge, MA: MIT Press.

Whiten, A., Custance, D. M., Gómez, J. C., Teixidor, P., & Bard, K. A. (1996). Imitative learning of artificial fruit processing in children (*Homo sapiens*) and chimpanzees (*Pan troglodytes*). *Journal of Comparative Psychology*, **110**, 3–14.

Whiten, A., Horner, V., Litchfield, C., & Marshall-Pescini, S. (2004). How do apes ape? *Learning and Behaviour*, **32**, 36–52.

Wimmer, H., & Perner, J. (1983). Beliefs about beliefs: Representation and constraining function of wrong beliefs in young children's understanding of deception. *Cognition*, **13**, 103–128.

Wittgenstein, L. (1955). *Philosophical investigations*. Oxford: Blackwell.

Woodward, A. (1998). Infants selectively encode the goal object of an actor's reach. *Cognition*, **69**, 1–34.

Woodward, A. (1999). Infants ability to distinguish between purposeful and non-purposeful behaviors. *Infant Behavior and Development*, **22** (2), 145–160.

Wrangham, R. W. (1980). An ecological model of female-bonded primate groups. *Behaviour*, **75** (3-sup-4), 262–300.

Wrangham, R. (in press). *The cooking ape*.

Zentall, T. (1996). An analysis of imitative learning in animals. In C. M. Heyes & B. G. Galef, Jr. (Eds.), *Social learning in animals: The roots of culture*. New York: Academic Press.

ACKNOWLEDGMENTS

Our thanks go first and foremost to Hanna Petschauer, who expertly organized and coordinated the data collection, coding, and collation. Thanks also to Susanne Mauritz, who played a very important role in the same activities in the later phases of the project. The study could not have been done without the dedication of the animal caretakers at the Wolfgang Köhler Primate Research Center throughout, but especially in helping to conduct the actual studies with our energetic subjects: Evelyn Kanzler, Daniela Rogge, Kerstin Schuldei, and Erika Seres. Daniel Stahl provided expert help with the statistics (though he is not to be blamed for our choice to do some parametric statistics with $n = 3$). Also thanks to Dorit Mersmann, David Buttlemann, Hagen Lehmann, Sara Hastings, Ivonne Geiger, and Birte Hey, for help with data collection and coding.

For correspondence contact either author at: Max Planck Institute for Evolutionary Anthropology, Deutscher Platz 6, D-04103 Leipzig, Germany. E-mail: tomas@eva.mpg.de; carpenter@eva.mpg.de

COMMENTARY

SOCIAL ENGAGEMENT AND UNDERSTANDING IN CHIMPANZEES AND HUMANS

R. Peter Hobson

It is difficult to write a commentary on a *Monograph* with which one is in substantial agreement. The dangers are twofold. On the one hand, a commentator might highlight strengths and end up doing little more than bouncing off an echo of the original text. On the other, he could exaggerate issues of difference where the underlying distinctions are less than impressive, and lapse into quibbling. Therefore I shall have to take care, because I do agree with much in the theoretical perspective elaborated by Tomasello and Carpenter. I shall try to fulfil my function of setting their arguments and findings in broader developmental context by noting just a few methodological points, and then dwelling on what I take to be subtle but important theoretical issues.

METHODOLOGICAL ISSUES

Tomasello and Carpenter are forthright about the limitations of their studies. They are explicit about the caveats and qualifications that must attend the business of drawing conclusions about chimpanzees in general, from studies that are limited to three and a half individuals of the species.

They have good reason to take this stance. There are special difficulties when the chimpanzees in question are raised in atypical circumstances, having been rejected by their mothers and raised partly by humans and partly in the company of other orphans. Just as one might argue that all the human input would have accustomed the chimpanzees to people and their experimental maneuverings and have fostered their social abilities to an optimal degree, it is also open to skeptics to wonder if this is really the best way to study the most that chimpanzees can achieve by way of social engagement and social cognition. No wonder if critics were to raise objections that even human infants wrested from their mothers at an early age and nurtured by members of another species might respond to experimental conditions in ways that are far from typical of their species.

Personally, I am not drawn to such skepticism, but it is also of note that in the present instance, a substantial part of the evidence concerns what these chimpanzees *failed* to do by way of picking up actions from humans in imitation, or how they *failed* to relate to humans in ways that indicate abilities to co-ordinate attention or to shift in collaborative and/or communicative roles. It is worth remembering that lack of evidence is not the same as evidence of lack. In one of these studies, for example, there was indeed a lack of evidence the chimpanzees showed understanding "that perceivers can focus their attention on one thing, or one aspect of a thing, within their perceptual fields for a reason." But to state that they "showed no understanding that perceivers can focus their attention . . . (etc)" is to put the matter rather forcefully.

It is always hazardous to make claims that individuals are unable to do this or that, when there are a host of potential reasons for a lack of responding. Tomasello and Carpenter do their best to cover themselves by arguing that their evidence is in keeping with other observational and experimental evidence on the abilities and limitations of chimpanzees. Yet on the matter of negative evidence, the best guarantee against mistakenly attributing lack of ability or engagement in a situation is to demonstrate that in closely related control conditions with alteration in some critical feature of the task, participants in the study do respond appropriately. Even when results seem to suggest an ability is present rather than absent, the evidence becomes persuasive only when profiles of performance across the various task conditions are in keeping with expectation, for example, when participants achieve higher scores on what are supposed to be the easiest conditions.

In these respects, Tomasello and Carpenter sometimes fail to deliver the *coup de gras*. In the test of copying style, for example, it is disconcerting that the "manipulation control" condition did not produce baseline scores for target result and style, so we are not clear what was happening here, nor whether some imitation of style in the test conditions might have been obscured. Also note that elsewhere, we were asked to accept partial forms of action as the full action, and I wonder how partial forms of style might have been rated. It is a pity that the study did not incorporate *contrasts* in style that could be discerned or rated as absent, rather than assessing the presence or absence of style according to somewhat arbitrary criteria (we did not learn how "attempts" to imitate style differed from successful imitation, nor whether these were counted as successes). It is interesting that two out of the three chimpanzees actually did produce more, albeit in the case of Alex only one more, instances of copying style in the immediate than in the manipulation condition, and none produced fewer; and it would have been helpful to know the proportion of times that style was imitated when target actions were actually performed, given that failures to copy the actions at all might well have reduced the likelihood of stylistic imitation.

What of the study of role-reversal? Here one critical component of the response, namely handing an object to the experimenter, was observed relatively often. Yet this was disqualified as a criterion for role-reversal on the basis of the facts that the chimpanzees received encouragement, and that an aspect of nonverbal communication (looking at the experimenter) that would signify offering was missing. Yet we do not have evidence from a control condition, that such looking occurred as a part of offering behavior when there was no requirement to reverse roles. Evidence of an absence of role-reversing that did not involve offering was described in outline only. Therefore it remains to confirm that offering-with-looking was a good index of role-reversal in the present context, or indeed, that this study tested anything beyond qualities of "offering" *per se.*

When we turn to consider the basis for imputing *success* in the various tasks, concern shifts to the possibility that the criteria are over-generous. In the case of responding to failed attempts, for example, it is curious that the chimpanzees were not consistent in copying the full completed target actions, and this makes one uncertain how to interpret their (none-too-striking) propensity to copy intended-but-not-completed actions. In the tests of understanding accidents, "attempts and partial actions (i.e., more than just touching the object) were included as reproductions"—but was this justified, when the point is whether the chimpanzees were imitating goal-directed-actions-as-intended, rather than partial forms of action that might be copied without reference to the agent's intention? In the first test of gaze-following, what might it tell us that there was a mean latency of over 25 seconds before a chimpanzee looked to where the experimenter was gazing behind a barrier, even though the experimenter was grunting and alternating gaze and calling the chimpanzee's name? It would appear that such evidence from so few participants is highly suggestive but not decisive.

Having registered these niggling uncertainties, I can launch into matters of theory.

LEVELS OF UNDERSTANDING

Tomasello and Carpenter write: "The question of chimpanzee social cognition should therefore not be phrased as whether chimpanzees do or do not have a "theory of mind," but rather how chimpanzees understand the other social beings that make up their social worlds in all of their many dimensions."

Quite so. And we find that the term "understanding" (or occasionally, "knowing") crops up again and again in the *Monograph*. All the more disconcerting, therefore, that the authors pay so little attention to the issue of "*how* chimpanzees understand . . . ," that is, what *understanding* or *knowing* mean in each of the contexts in which these terms are employed.

It is not an option to shrug off complexities in the development of understanding or knowledge, any more than one can shrug off complexities in the development of social relations and the ways these configure a child's or a chimpanzee's ways of relating to things and events in the environment. For example, we need to distinguish when and how the various biologically prepared mechanisms underlying perception and action and feeling and (in due course) thought come online in development, and when these mechanisms become integrated and transcended so that the individual acquires understanding of the world and the self in relation to that world.

Consider the case of a 2-month-old infant who responds in a qualitatively different way to a human being and some object approaching, as famously illustrated by Brazelton, Koslowski, and Main (1974). Clearly the infant discriminates the person from the thing, and the nature of this discrimination is such that the child shows different qualities of relatedness in both action and attitude. It is not unreasonable to think in terms of mechanisms within the child that promote orientation toward specific features of a person's body and behavior, and recruitment of those systems of the brain and body that engage feelings and result in patterns of personal relatedness and interpersonal coordination. It is equally fruitful to study the mechanisms for engaging the child's orientation and action readiness in relation to objects. Yet few people would want to say that these mechanisms understand anything (although it surprises me how many psychologists seem to be at ease in talking about innate knowledge). On the other hand, who would want to take issue with a person in the street who expresses delight that already a 2-month-old infant shows that she knows what a person is? So our familiar ways of talking about such goings-on may obscure developmental issues of great importance.

There is, of course, a well-trodden intellectual path from which we observe the distinction between implicit and explicit knowledge. Piaget (1972) was exercised in evolving a developmental account of the processes through which sensori-motor coordinations yield new forms of understanding of means-ends relations, object permanence, and so on, and he grappled with the task of explaining the emergence of the semiotic function. Karmiloff-Smith's (1992) thesis of representational redescription as a developmental process that yields higher-order modes of thinking falls in the same tradition. What I want to stress in the present context, are the potential pitfalls in collapsing different modes or qualities of social understanding.

There are two reasons why this is especially important when considering the emergence of social cognition. Firstly, we are trying to characterize the content of what is registered and reacted-to in the social domain—if you like, the "what" that affects an individual's responses to and engagement with another person—and at the same time, to specify the forms of cognitive activity or representation that encompass such content in different phases of development, the psychological means through which the individual is dealing with what is perceived and experienced. At any given point in time, even when we feel confident that we have identified a social phenomenon (such as sharing forms of joint attention), we may find we need to entertain rather than foreclose doubt about the nature of any understanding that appears to be manifest in those phenomena. Such understanding may be *neither* simply implicit *nor* yet explicit in nature.

Secondly, and critically, there is likely to be an especially intimate connection between the qualitative content of social experience early in life, and the development of the means by which higher forms of thinking (or representation) about that content are achieved. More specifically, I want to argue, a pivotal difference between chimpanzees and human beings is the way in which, as well as the degree to which, individuals apprehend a subjective dimension behind observable behavior in conspecifics. The quality of this *engagement with* the subjective orientation of others is what provides necessary conditions for the development of new levels of understanding and thinking about persons and minds.

If there is a kind of understanding that is neither simply implicit, nor clearly explicit, then what is it? Or correspondingly, if there is a way of responding to others that is neither automatic, nor represented *to* oneself in a conceptually emancipated form (e.g., in such a way as to be reflected upon and entertained as a topic for further thought), then how are we to characterize this mode of relatedness—and how should we decide if it is something chimpanzees and humans share? There are empirical and conceptual dimensions to these rhetorical questions. If as developmental psychologists, we can achieve a picture of the course and mechanisms of development, then we shall be in a position to frame concepts adequate to translate that picture into theoretically articulated form. On the other hand, it will help to interpret the empirical findings at hand, and to devise further studies, if we free ourselves from the constraints of inappropriate ways of thinking about our domain of study.

Here is the crux. I believe we should avoid drawing so absolute a distinction between observing behavior and apprehending the mind that underlies behavior. It is not merely that it is a matter of degree, how far we may take the stance of the detached watcher of actions or even the inspector of bodies—like a surgeon, say, or a sculptor—or instead, have the experience of relating to someone else in whose subjective life we participate. It is also that what we can observe from a relatively detached vantage-point, alongside our being involved with the other person, alters with development. Indeed, there are forms of detachment *from* our immediate engagement with others and the world that depend on our involvement *with* others and the world. In particular, it is through engagement with others' attitudes that we are moved to adopt the attitudes of others as "other" and yet now our own, assimilating such orientations as possibilities for our own relations to objects and events (including ourselves). Through our relations with others' ways of relating to a shared world, that is, we are lifted from a one-track mode of perceiving and relating to things, and acquire the capacity to move among different person-anchored perspectives. This mode of distancing and abstraction is a profoundly important social-development route to adopting an overview of the relations among self, other, and the world (Hobson, 1993a; 2002/2004).

So we need to appreciate that in early human development, there is a process that leads from prototypically implicit "understanding" of persons (for which probably we should retain quotation marks if we are to use the word "understanding" at all), to the acquisition of conceptually instantiated, mentally combinable and contrastable cognitive vehicles of understanding epitomized by linguistically formulated ideas concerning mental states. In one sense, this process *from* "understanding"-in-action and "understanding"-in-attitude *to* understanding-in-reflective-thought (and vice versa) can happen in adults as in children, a fact exploited in such cultural endeavors as art criticism. But as my reference to language suggests, the most important time for the development of this new level and quality of reflective understanding—involving some understanding of one's own understanding—occurs over the period between nine and (say) 20 months in typically developing children. If this is so, then it matters for evaluating what is similar and what is different between chimpanzees and children of this young age.

DEVELOPING UNDERSTANDING OF OTHERS' MINDS

It is not that Tomasello and Carpenter are oblivious to these issues. They reflect on the fact that certain aspects of mentality have a higher degree of behavioral expression than others, and write: ". . . we may posit that all primates naturally perceive and understand the basics of goal-directed action and perception based on consistent observable accompaniments and indications. . . ." Setting aside the problems with that word "understand," I agree. Children with autism can also perceive goal-directed actions, without this meaning they are very engaged with the person whose actions they are. Along parallel lines, I have suggested that we should consider how children's developing understanding of the mind moves from immediate apprehension of perceptible bodily expressed attitudes to a conceptual grasp of a person's subjective experiences and psychological stances (such as those of belief) that have more complex expressions in behavior (e.g., Hobson, 1993b). But my point here is that this also raises the question of what do we mean when we say that chimpanzees understand failed attempts and accidents? How do we think such understanding operates?

It is not at all obvious that we should leap to saying that chimpanzees understand "goals as internal representations," and I am not even clear how literally we are supposed to take this proposition. On the one hand, we might want to say that they recognize a different kind of action, but of course that begs the question of what a "different kind" might mean; on the other, we could imagine they can sense something of the bodily expressed attitudes that surround an action, and register that in the case of failed attempts and actions, this betrays their altered meaning; or on yet another hand, we might want to go further down the path to attributing some form of understanding such as might be linguistically formulated in terms of what the other was trying to do.

The importance of mapping out the many possibilities is not simply to characterize the abilities of chimpanzees and/or human infants. It is also that we might be helped to see how the very ambiguities and half-way cases hold the key to the nature of early development in children's understanding of the mind. The reason is that young children may pass through a succession of phases in which the source of their social abilities is neither wholly responsiveness to behavior in some physicalistic sense, nor wholly sensitivity to another's mental orientation (if ever there were such a thing, when responding to behavior always enters the picture). Rather, there is a shift over time as the mental vis-à-vis bodily *aspect* of intentional relations progressively colours a child's understanding. In due course, the child acquires new understandings of subjective life that depend less on what is immediately perceptible in behaviour. Probably, some of these new understandings involve conceptual growth that is relatively step-wise, for example when a child comes to understand belief in terms of *reality*-as-construed (where in my view, the contrast between appearance and reality, and the acquisition of a new concept of "reality," is critical).

So I tend to resist the choice between just two options, for example either that organisms are reacting with an automatic head-turn in response to another person's bodily orientation, or that they "understand that others see things and that if they look in that direction they will see what the others see." I think the range of possibilities is greater, and the less clear-cut cases are especially interesting if we want to understand development.

An example may illustrate what is at stake here. Consider the following quote from Wittgenstein:

> "I see that the child wants to touch the dog, but doesn't dare." How can I see that?—Is this description of what is seen on the same level as a description of moving shapes and colours? Is an interpretation in question? Well, remember that you may also *mimic* a human being who would like to touch something, but doesn't dare.

Wittgenstein is pointing out something relevant for how we interpret the actions of others at any given point in time, but also relevant for our developmental theorizing about social cognition. Is the *basis* for our understanding that we can infer the intentions of the other, or *a fortiori*, that we "understand goals as internal representations"? Or is it that in early development, as often in adulthood, an individual's ability to identify with (and potentially mimic) the state of someone else is basic? If the latter is correct, we can begin to trace how over the early years of life, apprehending and interiorizing another person's attitudes is transformed into comprehending mental states in terms of concepts of intentions, goals, mistakes, beliefs, and so on.

When we consider chimpanzees' reactions to failed attempts and accidents, then, we might ask: Are the chimpanzees identifying with, or even focusing upon, *an agent* when they respond to failed attempts and accidents? Or might there be other ways to register when *actions* fail to reach completion, and/or to detect signs that actions are not directed in the customary way? Is the nature of chimpanzees' understanding of such events really so similar to that of young children? This is an issue to which I shall return.

I–THOU AND I–IT RELATIONS

There is a long tradition of distinguishing between two developmental lines in early human mental growth: essentially, what Buber (1937/1984) was highlighting in his distinction between I–Thou and I–It relations. Aspects of this contrast have been incorporated into the theoretical approaches of developmentalists such as Bower (1979) and Trevarthen (1982), amongst many others. In more recent times, much has been written not only on the special qualities of I–Thou relatedness, but also the significance of such relatedness for the development of understanding and knowledge of minds (e.g., Hamlyn, 1978; Hobson, 1993a, b).

More than this, it has become apparent that even *within* the domain of social interaction and relationships, some aspects of person–perception and responsiveness are saturated with I–Thou (intersubjective) qualities, and some are not. The study of autism has been especially illuminating here. For example, Moore, Hobson, and Lee (1997; and Hobson, 1995, for a theoretical perspective) provided evidence that children with autism are relatively adept at perceiving and recognizing actions in point-light displays of people shown on videotape, but very limited in recognizing subjective and emotional states. Whereas participants with autism were likely to comment on a point-light person "scratching," for example, matched participants without autism would tend to say the person was "itching." This group contrast was apparent both when participants gave responses to the open question: "What is happening here?," and when (in another condition, with tasks that were adjusted for levels of difficulty) they were probed more specifically for the accuracy with which they could judge what the depicted person was doing on the one hand, or feeling on the other. Complementary evidence suggests that although children with autism can read the intentions of other people (e.g., Carpenter, Pennington, & Rogers, 2001), they are relatively limited in their awareness and/or responsiveness to other people's attitudes (e.g., Sigman, Kasari, Kwon, & Yirmiya, 1992). Our theoretical point was that perception of and engagement with subjective states is specifically impaired in autism, and specifically related to these children's limitations in conceptualizing minds.

Presumably, Tomasello and Carpenter were not persuaded by this evidence, for they state that the change in their views about the insufficiency of reading intentions for social-cognitive development was prompted by recent research on primates' ability to interpret goal-directed actions. In any case, the upshot is that there are dissociable lines of development in perceiving and understanding goal-directed actions on the one hand, and perceiving and understanding bodily manifest subjective states on the other. It appears that whatever the role of reading intentions—and this may be a substantial role—there is something about an individual's perception of and responsiveness to attitudes that is critical for coming to develop increasingly sophisticated concepts about people's minds.

I find it curious that despite their emphasis on the business of sharing in early development, Tomasello and Carpenter are able to write: "Understanding others in this way, as intentional agents, is the foundation for all other forms of social understanding in the sense that we actually define what a person is doing by the goals she is trying to achieve." If they mean understanding of persons as agents who have intentional relations with the world—that is, who have intentional mental states (not merely who intend to act) and experience the world as falling under such-and-such a description for the person whose experience it is—this is a justifiable claim. But understanding these kinds of intentional relations require far more than reading the intentions behind others' actions, and sometimes the far more that is involved seems to recede into the theoretical background. *Do* we define what a person is doing *simply* in terms of the goals she is trying to achieve—and insofar as we do, does this not presuppose a great deal in what we understand about her psychological orientation? Now and again I feel uncertain what Tomasello and Carpenter are claiming *is* foundational for all other forms of social understanding.

Perhaps the issues will become clearer if we consider the difference between understanding "what a person is *doing*" and "what a *person* is doing."

UNDERSTANDING ACTIONS AND UNDERSTANDING PERSONS

I have already remarked that in whatever way chimpanzees do discriminate failed attempts and accidents from intended actions, this may not mean that the quality of their understanding of others as agents is the same as that of young children who respond similarly in the tasks. And even *if* chimpanzees have what might be called "understanding," this may be an understanding of the structure and concomitants of *actions*, but entail relatively little understanding about the nature of the *person* or agent who intends those actions. As I have indicated, there is much more to understanding others as intentional agents than seeing their behavior as goal-directed, even if one restricts the notion of "intentional" to the domain of intending-to-act. More than this, a chimpanzee may perceive how actions are goal-directed, without having the kind of orientation toward or understanding of the other person that is required for a grasp of what it means to intend-to-act like I (as a person) intend to act.

Tomasello and Carpenter write: "One interpretation of this pattern of observations is that although apes know that others have goals and perceptions, they have little desire to share them." Again setting aside what "know" (and especially, "know that") means here, there is the question of whether it would be correct to characterize such knowledge as encompassing what "others have" by way of intentional mental states. This way of putting things suggests that knowledge is in place about the nature of persons, but motivation to share is lacking. I would put it another way. Perhaps it is that apes can respond to behavior in such a way that the goals-in-action and directedness-in-orientation are registered, but that their lack of the desire to share is not so much a lack of desiring to share "them" (viz. goals and perceptions), but rather, a deeper lack of intersubjective engagement with others that is *also* manifest in a lack of understanding that goals and perceptions exist *as characteristics of persons*. If I am right, we should not be drawing boxes of what chimpanzees understand to be happening in people's heads (or hearts).

To take another example, Tomasello and Carpenter write: "Chimpanzees' analysis of goal-directed action, then, may operate mainly on the level of the internal goal the actor is striving to achieve; chimpanzees may not delve deeper into the rational dimensions of the process to explain why actors chose the means that they did in pursuing their goal." But perhaps this lack of delving is unsurprising if it is *not* at the level of an internal goal that a chimpanzee is analyzing. For a chimpanzee to apprehend that a goal was not achieved through actions is not the same as understanding "that the demonstrator had a goal that was not achieved." The person-focus that we maintain in *our* understanding, and the person-anchorage of mental states that we respect, may not feature to a human-like degree in whatever understanding chimpanzees achieve. Why? Because they are less engaged with the person, and there are other ways to understand action, even action that is not effective in accomplishing its goal. Again I hesitate to follow the jump from statements about chimpanzees responding to aspects of action, to statements about chimpanzees understanding how other persons (or individuals of other species) relate to or represent the world.

IMITATING STYLE

There is one other line of research in autism that is very relevant to the present discussion. This concerns the children's propensity and/or ability to copy other people. As cited by Tomasello and Carpenter, some years ago my colleague Tony Lee and I conducted a study in which we demonstrated that children with autism are relatively adept at copying goal-directed actions, but are markedly less likely than matched children without autism to imitate styles of action (mainly but not exclusively, harsh vs. gentle versions of actions), or to imitate the other's orientation-of-action-toward-himself by orientating the copied action toward themselves (Hobson & Lee, 1999). We interpreted the findings in terms of the children with autism being able to *copy goal-directed actions* but failing to *imitate and appropriate a person's* style and self-orientation.

Contrast our theoretical stance with that underpinning the study of chimpanzees' propensity to imitate style in the present *Monograph*. Tomasello and Carpenter state that in order "to test the ability (or motivation) to go down a level in the behavioral hierarchy to others' sub-goals and means, we investigated the tendency to copy the particular "style" others use when acting."

I think Tomasello and Carpenter underestimate what is at stake here. It is not merely that the human child who imitates style is noticing or interpreting something about sub-goals and means. It is also that she aligns herself with the bodily expressive stance of the other, and makes something of the other's orientation-in-acting her own. To anticipate later discussion, what notions of representation-plus-motivation do we need to capture this? I do not dismiss the important fact that early in life, we come to represent ourselves-in-relation-to-others and others-in-relation-to-ourselves, and also incorporate the external world in these representations. *A fortiori*, I do not underestimate that we are motivated to engage with others, or that others "move" us to assume their attitudes. What I do question, is whether Tomasello and Carpenter are thinking about the imitation of style in an appropriate frame of reference.

To put it briefly: I think there is a way in which picking up styles of action is deeply connected with picking up emotional attitudes. In each case, a person can (in part) assume the orientation of the other, in a way that may or may not be manifest in immediate actions or feelings. This is happening all the time in our interpersonal exchanges, only sometimes beneath the surface and disclosed at a later time, if at all. When we *identify with* another person, we both register and interiorize the other's orientation, as if from the other person's stance—and this happens through the way we perceive that psychological stance as bodily expressed. Note it is also possible to imitate someone else performing actions through identification, but critical here is the process through which the imitation takes place, because actions can be copied through processes that do *not* involve identification. In the paradigmatic case of imitating a person's style of action, the imitation entails something more like being moved to assume the other's emotional/subjective orientation, rather than copying action from an external viewpoint—unless, that is, style is presented as a goal-to-be-copied, as in our most recent studies, when it *can* be copied from a detached point of view. But as an important post-script, note that there are two rather different ways to resonate to feelings and to imitate style, as well as to pick up other bodily expressions such as gestures or postures: firstly, through a process that is automatic and achieves immediate psychological linkage with the other, and secondly, as in deliberate and intended acts of empathy or copying.

MECHANISMS OF DEVELOPMENT

Tomasello and Carpenter stress the significance of young children's ability to achieve a "bird's eye view" of interpersonal collaboration "in which all components are within a single representational format—which constitutes a dialogic cognitive representation." In this regard, they are appropriately hesitant about the developmental story. On the one hand, they consider the possibility that the "sharing of psychological states engaged in by human infants and caregivers is internalised and cognitively represented, in Vygotskian fashion, so creating dialogic cognitive representations." On the other hand, they consider whether organisms might have special forms of representation, as well as special social motivation, as biological givens. Alongside all of this, they half-reject the notion that processes of identification might provide what is needed for an adequate explanation, "certainly not if we mean bodily identification."

In this latter phrase, Tomasello and Carpenter erect a straw man. To my knowledge, no one has suggested that identification is simply a bodily matter, and (happily) Tomasello and Carpenter appear to leave open the issue of whether "a more deeply psychological level of identification with others" could hold the key to the phylogenetic and ontogenetic stories (Hobson, 2002/2004). But before I come to that, what are we trying to explain?

Take the issue of how infants come to share experiences (Hobson, 1989). It is essential to the meaning of what it is to share, that one individual connects with someone else in sharing *a subjective orientation*. Inevitably, again we are faced with the need to characterize different levels as well as degrees of sharing, so that there is a case to say that anything like a typically human form of sharing entails sharing awareness of the sharing (Meyer, 2003, personal communication, cited in Hobson, 2005). An account of the development of more cognitively elaborated forms of sharing will implicate an account of the development of self- and other-awareness. It is only in a metaphorical sense that one might talk of two tuning-forks sharing a given frequency of oscillation, and for interpersonal sharing, there needs to be self-other differentiation as well as self-other connectedness and commonality in subjective state.

So ... does sharing itself require special forms of motivation and cognitive representation, and how are we to explain the derivation of more elaborate self-other-world understanding?

There are two ways to interpret the claim that one needs a special motivation alongside a form of new representation. The one is to suppose we need two different things in the mental economy, a motivation and a species of representation. The other is to suppose that there is one process that distinguishes sharing in human infants and (relatively) limited sharing in chimpanzees, and this process has affective and motivational and cognitive manifestations and consequences. If the internalization and cognitive representation of sharing *creates* dialogic cognitive representations, then dialogic representations cannot be the means by which sharing is experienced and internalized. We are left with the challenge of characterizing the

145

psychological structures implicated in sharing. On the other hand, if dialogic representations are required for sharing (and this does not seem to be the view of Tomasello and Carpenter), then how do such representations come into existence, and how are they configured—and what makes them representations?

It is here that the concept of identification enters the picture. My proposal is this. Firstly, over the early months of life, and probably according to a biologically constrained and relatively experience-independent process, human beings manifest a propensity to respond to the bodily expressions of other people with coordinated experiences of their own. The various components of primary intersubjectivity—attentiveness to faces and gestural meanings, coordinated timing of interaction, and so on—each play a role in bringing this about. Here is a set of events that we might describe from the point of view of perception, affect, will, or cognition, and the fact that we can apply these descriptions is important from a developmental point of view. For this terminological fact is connected with another, developmental fact: what happens at this early stage in the form of configurations of personal relatedness will have profound developmental implications for later nonsocial as well as social perception, affect, motivation, and cognition.

The process of identification may or may not need representations, but it does involve the infant with others in powerful ways. Sure enough, this means that the propensity to coordinate and connect with other humans—the draw to intersubjectivity, the motivation to share—is especially strong in human beings. The very fact of apprehending and participating in another person's emotional life, of being moved by the other, *is* motivational. In addition to this, identification is a process in which the individual *registers*, and in due course comes to represent, the otherness of the other as part of the experience, as well as self-centered aspects of the resulting phenomenal state. In other words, it makes a difference that the experience is one occurring in the context of self–other personal relatedness, even though to begin with, self and other are not conceptualized. This is merely to explicate the grounds for supposing that even in the early months of life, the infant is indeed sharing experiences with someone else.

It is important that none of this presupposes a degree of understanding of what another human being is. What it does presuppose, is that the infant has the perceptual-affective-motivational propensities to seek out, register, and respond to other human beings in special ways that result in interpersonal linkage. At the same time, there needs to be a boundary within the infant's experience, of what does and what does not have its source in another experienced as separable from the self. As an aside, it may be noted that insofar as humans are grouped as humans and not things (more or less, given that one can deceive infants by presenting them with human-like forms), this achievement might be thought of as a cognitive operation, even if its source is affective-relational.

As if this is not enough, sharing presupposes something else. I have suggested that the infant experiences the other person's bodily-manifest attitudes and relational engagement with herself. The paradox is that the infant has two forms of experience within one form of experience. She has her own anticipations of and reactions to the other, and then her experience of these states as being either complemented by, or out of keeping with, another set of experiences—again, *her* experiences—derived from and experienced in the context of what she perceives in the other.

What is the evidence for this account? The most widely-cited studies are those demonstrating neonatal imitation of tongue-protrusion, mouth opening, hand gestures, and facial expressions (e.g., Meltzoff & Moore, 1977; Field, Woodson, Greenberg, & Cohen, 1982), and these do speak to the claim that another person's actions are registered as "other." It is especially striking how the neonate who imitates in this setting gradually approximates her action to the model of the other. But arguably, this is tangential to claims about the structure of *intersubjective* coordination. So consider a case example, that of a typically developing 2-month-old whom we videotaped in a standard still-face situation with her mother. When the mother assumed the still-face and unreactive posture as requested, the infant responded by becoming uneasy, restless, and jerky in her movements, and lost the infectious smiling and smooth tonguing movements that had been evident just moments before. Her bright, protracted gazes into her mother's eyes were transformed into brief, checking glances. More important for the present purposes, after about 40 seconds her behavior changed again, and she began to give longer looks *to her mother* accompanied by forced smiles. There was a strong impression that she was seeking to reestablish contact with her mother, trying to elicit a resumption of the joyful interpersonal exchange that was now missing.

If all this is correct, then we see how the infant participates in experience *with* the other. Sharing experience with someone else is not merely like having one's own experience of the world, and then adding something. It seems more like having one's own subjective state *and* registering something of the other's attitudes conjointly, in a qualitatively new form of experience (also Tronick & Members of the Boston Change Process Study Group, 1998).

I do not know whether it is appropriate to call this a dialogic experience. Perhaps that doesn't matter. What does matter is that it is not merely the motivation to share, but also the biologically based propensity to experience attitudes through others and to achieve a kind of partitioning, or differentiation-cum-linkage, based on the sources of those attitudes.

Why this matters is that it provides a necessary condition for the progressive elaboration of understandings about self and other. Development proceeds not by starting with self-experience and then imputing similar experiences to others, but with sharing experiences and then achieving new understandings of what belongs to self and what to another person (Barresi & Moore, 1996). The understandings transform cognition in the nonsocial as well as the social domain. In due course, but not until the second year of life, self and other are conceptualized as persons with minds.

SIMULATION AND "THEORY THEORY"

This brings me to a final item on the agenda: the claim that we understand others' minds on the basis of simulating their experiences. Sometimes this view is pitted against a "theory theory" account of interpersonal understanding. In my view, accounts of each variety have captured something of the truth, but most versions of each are importantly misleading.

The problem with one current form of simulation account—and I am concerned that there are hints of this in the present *Monograph*, when Tomasello and Carpenter suggest that "infants *use* their own experience to simulate that of others" (my italics)—is that the course of development is said to lead from awareness of one's own states, to understanding the states of others. It is supposed that one comes to attribute mental states to others, by a process of simulation and then ascription by analogy. I can conceptualize my own states, I can observe you and simulate your states, and as a result I can ascribe mental states to you. The weaknesses of this position were exposed by Wittgenstein (1958; also Carpendale & Lewis, 2004). We cannot identify our own experiences as of such-and-such a kind unless we already share a form of life with others, and come to agreement in judgments about mental states that have both external manifestations and an internal, subjective quality.

The theory theory is prone to a complementary set of difficulties, many of which I have discussed elsewhere (e.g., Hobson, 1991). Here there is a tendency to underestimate the requirement that in order for theory (or better, concepts) of mind to acquire cognitive structure as well as content, we need pre-theoretical and affective foundations in the experience of interpersonal relations. As developmental psychologists, we need to explain how humans come to understand the nature of people whose minds find bodily expression—necessarily, since there is much about the mind that is perceptible in behavior—and connect a person to his or her world. Talk of representations and metarepresentations is all very well, but these are the servants and not the masters of interpersonal understanding. Concepts of mind are really important, but these are distillations and cognitive elaborations of what is experienced in our blood-and-guts emotional transactions with other persons.

I think the appropriate synthesis is as follows. Yes, there occur correspondences set up between an infant and other people's subjective states, from early in life; to be sure, these are pre-theoretical and *in one special sense* simulations, and by no means predominantly cognitive (insofar as this term has anything like a customary sense when applied to infancy); and beyond this, they provide essential ingredients for interpersonal understanding. It is not possible to imagine how one individual could conceptualize what it means to be a person with a mind and experiences, if that individual did not also have experiences that provide some of the content of what is understood. Computers never will understand human minds. On the other hand, a solipsist could not come to conceptualize his or her own mental states simply on the basis of his or her own experiences. In the elaborated sense in which simulation is often meant, where one individual has access to his or her own mind and can recognize this or that mental state, one needs to have conceptualized such states, and such conceptualization is the outcome of, not the basis for, interpersonal engagement and sensitivity to the subjective orientations of others. So yes, too, there is a story to tell about the emergence of the conceptual/theoretical means to understanding minds, a story that begins with pre-theoretical capacities to share and co-ordinate attitudes. Sharing and co-ordinating experiences are critical for acquiring mental state concepts of thinking, wishing, feeling, and the like that can be attributed *both* to the self *and* to other people (Strawson, 1962).

Understanding persons with minds is a complex developmental achievement. As Tomasello and Carpenter indicate, our task in characterizing the level and quality of this kind of "understanding" in chimpanzees involves far more than deciding whether or not they have a "theory of mind."

CONCLUSIONS

The empirical studies presented in this *Monograph* suggest that orphaned and largely human-reared chimpanzees show little evidence of sharing attention with humans, of imitating style, of orientating to a human being's focus on one aspect of a perceived situation, of responding to gestures as expressing communicative intent, or of achieving the kinds of role-reversal that are needed for truly collaborative acts. In contrast with this, chimpanzees make behavioral adjustments to failed attempts and accidental actions by humans, and do not respond as if these were intended. Here we see a dissociation akin to that already reported in individuals with autism, who perceive, recognize, and copy the goal-directed actions of others, but appear to be much less perceptive of, engaged with, and responsive to the bodily expressed attitudes, emotions and stylistic expressions of other people. Children with autism are limited in the degree to which they are moved by and into others' mental orientations—they rarely *identify with* others—and it is no wonder that not just their thinking about the mind, but also their thinking in nonsocial domains, is limited and often one-track in nature. So, too, it may be no coincidence that chimpanzees who fail to get far below the skin into the subjective lives of others are also deprived, by and large, of flexible conceptual/linguistic forms of thinking.

In theoretical orientation, Tomasello and Carpenter elaborate their own version of the distinction between two different developmental lines in the social-relational domain, and now find a prominent place for a specifically human quality of interpersonal emotional engagement in explaining early social-cognitive development. This substantially rebalances Tomasello's (1999) earlier view of the developmental role of infants' ability to read intentions. It sets the stage for more detailed empirical and theoretical examination of how potentially dissociable social and nonsocial abilities are interwoven to yield the forms of understanding persons, but also the modes of truly understanding *anything*, that flower over the second year of life. Not only this, but the authors also offer us many interesting and engaging speculations about the evolutionary background to the growth of social cognition, for instance in their reflections on competition and collaboration.

Finally, there is the matter of giving a psychological account of the mechanisms of development in these domains. Perhaps it is becoming clearer that we need a framework within which we can track progressively elaborated forms of self/other differentiation and connectedness in the intersubjective domain, and appreciate how movements in attitudes *across* individuals, and correspondingly flexible stances in attitude within the individual's own mind (through a Vygotsky-like process of interiorization), are critical for cognitive as well as social development. To entertain perspectives as perspectives—or more accurately, to entertain a range of psychological orientations toward a world that includes oneself—is to be aware of oneself as an individual among others who can entertain perspectives. Awareness of one's own and others' minds is not so colorless a business as it sounds, for it involves being *engaged with* the attitudes of oneself and other people.

One of the great benefits of the present studies of chimpanzees, like studies of children with autism, is that they afford an opportunity to see how individuals who (for whatever reason) relatively lack the propensity to move into, and appropriate, the subjective stance of other individuals, also lack a powerful *impetus* and *means* to moving among alternative perspectives in their own minds. Perhaps most importantly for symbolic development, they miss a social-developmental trick that revolutionizes cognitive development: they fail to assume a halfway-external stance that would enable them to relate to their own relations with the world.

References

Barresi, J., & Moore, C. (1996). Intentional relations and social understanding. *Behavioral and Brain Sciences*, **19**, 107–154.

Brazelton, T. B., Koslowski, B., & Main, M. (1974). The origins of reciprocity: The early mother–infant interaction. In M. Lewis & L. A. Rosenblum (Eds.), *The effect of the infant on its caregiver* (pp. 49–76). New York, NY: Wiley.

Bower, T. G. R. (1979). *Human development*. San Francisco, CA: W.H. Freeman.

Buber, M. (1937/1984). *I and Thou* (2nd ed.) (Translated by R. G. Smith). Edinburgh: Clark.

Carpendale, J. I. M., & Lewis, C. (2004). Constructing an understanding of mind: The development of children's social understanding within social interaction. *Behavioral and Brain Sciences*, **27**, 79–151.

Carpenter, M., Pennington, B. F., & Rogers, S. J. (2001). Understanding of others' intentions in children with autism. *Journal of Autism and Developmental Disorders*, **31**, 589–599.

Field, T. M., Woodson, R., Greenberg, R., & Cohen, D. (1982). Discrimination and imitation of facial expressions by neonates. *Science*, **218**, 179–181.

Hamlyn, D. W. (1978). *Experience and the growth of understanding*. London: Routledge & Kegan Paul.

Hobson, R. P. (1989). On sharing experiences. *Development and Psychopathology*, **1**, 197–203.

Hobson, R. P. (1991). Against the theory of "Theory of Mind." *British Journal of Developmental Psychology*, **9**, 33–51.

Hobson, R. P. (1993a). *Autism and the development of mind*. Hove, Sussex: Erlbaum.

Hobson, R. P. (1993b). The emotional origins of social understanding. *Philosophical Psychology*, **6**, 227–249.

Hobson, R. P. (1995). Apprehending attitudes and actions: Separable abilities in early development? *Development and Psychopathology*, **7**, 171–182.

Hobson, R. P. (2002/2004). *The cradle of thought*. London/New York: Macmillan/Oxford University Press.

Hobson, R. P. (2005). What puts the jointness into joint attention? In N. Eilan, C. Hoerl, T. McCormack & J. Roessler (Eds.), *Joint attention: Communication and other minds* (pp. 185–204). Oxford: Clarendon.

Hobson, R. P., & Lee, A. (1999). Imitation and identification in autism. *Journal of Child Psychology and Psychiatry*, **40**, 649–659.

Karmiloff-Smith, A. (1992). *Beyond modularity: A developmental perspective on cognitive science*. Cambridge, MA: MIT Press.

Meltzoff, A. N., & Moore, M. K. (1977). Imitation of facial and manual gestures by human neonates. *Science*, **198**, 75–78.

Moore, D., Hobson, R. P., & Lee, A. (1997). Components of person perception: An investigation with autistic, nonautistic retarded and normal children and adolescents. *British Journal of Developmental Psychology*, **15**, 401–423.

Piaget, J. (1972). *The principles of genetic epistemology*. (Translated by W. Mays.) London: Routledge & Kegan Paul.

Sigman, M. D., Kasari, C., Kwon, J. H., & Yirmiya, N. (1992). Responses to the negative emotions of others by autistic, mentally retarded, and normal children. *Child Development*, **63**, 796–807.

Strawson, P. F. (1962, originally 1958). Persons. In V. C. Chappell (Ed.), *The philosophy of mind* (pp. 127–146). Englewood Cliffs, NJ: Prentice-Hall.

Tomasello, M. (1999). *The cultural origins of human cognition*. Cambridge, MA: Harvard University Press.

Trevarthen, C. (1982). The primary motives for cooperative understanding. In G. Butterworth & P. Light (Eds.), *Social cognition* (pp. 77–109). Brighton: Harvester.

Tronick, E. Z., & Members of the Boston Change Process Study Group (1998). Dyadically expanded states of consciousness and the process of therapeutic change. *Infant Mental Health Journal*, **19**, 290–299.

Wittgenstein, L. (1958). *Philosophical investigations*. (Translated by G. E. M. Anscombe.) Oxford: Blackwell.

Acknowledgment

I thank Dr. Jessica Meyer for her help in preparing this commentary.

CONTRIBUTORS

Michael Tomasello (Ph.D., 1980, Psychology, University of Georgia) taught at Emory University and worked at Yerkes Primate Center from 1980 to 1998. Since 1998, he is Co-Director at the Max Planck Institute for Evolutionary Anthropology, Leipzig, Germany. Research interests focus on processes of social cognition, social learning, and communication and language in human children and great apes. Books include *Primate Cognition* (w/J. Call, Oxford University Press, 1997), *The Cultural Origins of Human Cognition* (Harvard University Press, 1999), and *Constructing a Language: A Usage-Based Theory of Language Acquisition* (Harvard University Press, 2003).

Malinda Carpenter (Ph.D., 1995, Psychology, Emory University) currently is a member of the scientific staff of the Department of Developmental and Comparative Psychology at the Max Planck Institute for Evolutionary Anthropology. Her research interests include imitation and other types of social learning, infants' understanding of intentions and other mental states, and joint attention and other early social-cognitive skills. She has worked with typically developing infants and young children, young children with autism, and apes.

R. Peter Hobson (Ph.D., 1989, FRCPsych, CPsychol) is Tavistock Professor of Developmental Psychopathology in the University of London. He is an experimental psychologist and psychiatrist (and psychoanalyst), trained at Cambridge University and the Maudsley Hospital, London, and now at the Tavistock Clinic, London and the Institute of Child Health, University College, London. His primary research interest is the contribution of social relations to early cognitive as well as social development. His principal fields of study are early childhood autism, congenital blindness, mother–infant relations, and adult borderline personality disorder. His first book was entitled *Autism and the development of mind* (Erlbaum, 1993), and his second more accessible and wide-ranging book is called *The Cradle of Thought* (Oxford University Press, 2004).

STATEMENT OF EDITORIAL POLICY

The *Monographs* series is devoted to publishing developmental research that generates authoritative new findings and uses these to foster fresh, better integrated, or more coherent perspectives on major developmental issues, problems, and controversies. The significance of the work in extending developmental theory and contributing definitive empirical information in support of a major conceptual advance is the most critical editorial consideration. Along with advancing knowledge on specialized topics, the series aims to enhance cross-fertilization among developmental disciplines and developmental sub fields. Therefore, clarity of the links between the specific issues under study and questions relating to general developmental processes is important. These links, as well as the manuscript as a whole, must be as clear to the general reader as to the specialist. The selection of manuscripts for editorial consideration, and the shaping of manuscripts through reviews-and-revisions, are processes dedicated to actualizing these ideals as closely as possible.

Typically *Monographs* entail programmatic large-scale investigations; sets of programmatic interlocking studies; or—in some cases—smaller studies with highly definitive and theoretically significant empirical findings. Multi-authored sets of studies that center on the same underlying question can also be appropriate; a critical requirement here is that all studies address common issues, and that the contribution arising from the set as a whole be unique, substantial, and well integrated. The needs of integration preclude having individual chapters identified by individual authors. In general, irrespective of how it may be framed, any work that is judged to significantly extend developmental thinking will be taken under editorial consideration.

To be considered, submissions should meet the editorial goals of *Monographs* and should be no briefer than a minimum of 80 pages (including references and tables). There is an upper limit of 175–200 pages. In exceptional circumstances this upper limit may be modified. (Please submit four copies.) Because a *Monograph* is inevitably lengthy and usually substantively complex, it is particularly important that the text be well organized and written in clear, precise, and literate English. Note, however, that authors from non-English-speaking countries should not be put off by this stricture. In accordance with the general aims of SRCD, this series is actively interested in promoting international exchange of developmental research. Neither membership in the Society nor affiliation with the academic discipline of psychology are relevant in considering a *Monographs* submission.

The corresponding author for any manuscript must, in the submission letter, warrant that all coauthors are in agreement with the content of the manuscript. The corresponding author also is responsible for informing all coauthors, in a timely manner, of manuscript submission, editorial decisions, reviews received, and any revisions recommended. Before publication, the corresponding author also must warrant in the submission letter that the study has been conducted according to the ethical guidelines of the Society for Research in Child Development.

Potential authors who may be unsure whether the manuscript they are planning would make an appropriate submission are invited to draft an outline of what they propose, and send it to the Editor for assessment. This mechanism, as well as a more detailed description of all editorial policies, evaluation process, and format requirements can be found at the Editorial Office web site (http://astro.temple.edu/-overton/monosrcd.html) or by contacting the Editor, Wills F. Overton, Temple University-Psychology, 1701 North 13th St. – Rm 567, Philadelphia, PA 19122-6085 (e-mail: monosrcd@temple.edu) (telephone: 1-215-204-7360).

Monographs of the Society for Reasearch in Child Development (ISSN 0037-976X), one of two publications of Society of Research in Child Development, is published four times a year by Blackwell Publishing with offices at 350 Main St, Malden, MA 02148 USA and PO Box 1354, Garsington Rd, Oxford, OX4 2DQ, UK and PO Box 378 Carlton South, 3053 Victoria, Australia. A subscription to *Monographs of the SRCD* comes with a subscription to *Child Development* (published bimonthly).

INFORMATION FOR SUBSCRIBERS For new orders, renewals, sample copy requests, claims, changes of address and all other subscription correspondences please contact the Journals Department at your nearest Blackwell office (address details listed above). UK office phone: +44 (0) 1865-778315, Fax: +44 (0) 1865-471775, Email: customerservices@ oxon.blackwellpublishing.com; US office phone: 800-835-6770 or 781-388-8200, Fax: 781-388-8232, Email: subscrip@bos.blackwellpublishing.com; Asia office phone: +61 3 9347 0300, Fax: +61 3 9347 5001, Email: subscriptions@blackwellpublishingasia.com

INSTITUTIONAL PREMIUM RATES* FOR MONOGRAPHS OF THE SRCD/CHILD DEVELOPMENT 2005 The Americas $449, Rest of World £319. Customers in Canada should add 7% GST to The Americas price or provide evidence of entitlement to exemption. Customers in the UK and EU should add VAT at 5% or provide a VAT registration number or evidence of entitlement to exemption.

*Includes print plus premium online access to the current and all available backfiles. Print and online-only rates are also available.

BACK ISSUES Back issues are available from the publisher at the current single issue rate.

MICROFORM The journal is available on microfilm. For microfilm service, address inquiries to ProQuest Information and Learning, 300 North Zeeb Road, Ann Arbor, MI 48106-1346, USA. Bell and Howell Serials Customer Service Department: (800) 521-0600 × 2873.

ADVERTISING For advertising information, please visit the journal's website at www.blackwellpublishing.com/mono or contact the Academic and Science, Advertising Sales Coordinator, at journaladsUSA@bos.blackwellpublishing.com. 350 Main St. Malden, MA 02148. Phone: 781.388.8532, Fax: 781.338.8532.

MAILING Periodical postage paid at Boston, MA and additional offices. Mailing to rest of world by DHL Smart & Global Mail. Canadian mail is sent by Canadian publications mail agreement number 40573520. Postmaster: Send all address changes to Monographs of the Societey for Research in Child Development, Blackwell Publishing Inc., Journals Subscription Department, 350 Main St., Malden, MA 02148-5018.

Sign up to receive Blackwell *Synergy* free e-mail alerts with complete *Monographs of the SRCD* tables of contents and quick links to article abstracts from the most current issue. Simply go to www.blackwell synergy.com, select the journal from the list of journals, and click on "Sign-up" for FREE email table of contents alerts.

COPYRIGHT All rights reserved. With the exception of fair dealing for the purposes of research or private study, or criticism or review, no part of this publication may be reproduced, stored or transmitted in any form or by any means without the prior permission in writing from the copyright holder. Authorization to photocopy items for internal and personal use is granted by the copyright holder for libraries and other users of the Copyright Clearance Center (CCC), 222 Rosewood Drive, Danvers, MA 01923, USA (www.copy right.com), provided the appropriate fee is paid directly to the CCC. This consent does not extend to other kinds of copying, such as copying for general distribution for advertising or promotional purposes, for creating new collective works or for resale. For all other permissions inquiries, including requests to republish material in another work, please contact the Journals Rights & Permissions Coordinator, Blackwell Publishing, 9600 Garsington Road, Oxford OX4 2DQ, UK. Email: JournalsRights@oxon.blackwell publishing.com.

© 2005 Society for Research in Child Development